Industrial Cybersecurity and Operational Technology Security (OT)

James Relington

DEDICATION

This book is dedicated to all the professionals working tirelessly to secure digital identities and protect organizations from ever-evolving threats. To the cybersecurity teams, IT administrators, and identity management experts who ensure safe and seamless access for users— your work is invaluable. And to my family and friends, whose support and encouragement made this journey possible, thank you.

vi

AKNOWLEDGEMENTS

I would like to express my deepest gratitude to everyone who contributed to the creation of this book. To my colleagues and mentors in the cybersecurity and identity management field, your insights and expertise have been invaluable. To the organizations and professionals who shared their experiences and best practices, your contributions have enriched this work. A special thank you to my family and friends for their unwavering support and encouragement throughout this journey. Finally, to the readers, thank you for your interest in identity lifecycle management—may this book help you navigate the evolving landscape of digital security with confidence.

Introduction to Industrial and OT Cybersecurity

Cybersecurity has evolved over the past decades as a core discipline for protecting IT systems across multiple industries. However, in the industrial domain and in operational technology (OT) systems, the approach and challenges are different from those in information technology (IT). Unlike traditional IT systems, which focus on data management and information security, industrial environments rely on operational continuity and physical security, which entails different risks and threats.

OT systems encompass a wide range of technologies used in critical infrastructure, manufacturing, energy, transportation, and other industrial sectors. These include industrial control systems (ICS), such as SCADA systems, programmable logic controllers (PLCs), and power distribution systems. Security in these environments is crucial because any successful disruption or attack can have catastrophic consequences, including production stoppages, damage to expensive equipment, and even risks to human life.

One of the main challenges in OT cybersecurity is the convergence between industrial systems and IT networks. Historically, OT systems operated in isolated environments, with no direct connection to the Internet or external networks. However, with digital transformation and the adoption of technologies such as the Industrial Internet of Things (IIoT), cloud and real-time data analytics, these networks have begun to integrate with IT infrastructures. This has brought multiple benefits in terms of efficiency and optimization, but it has also exposed industrial systems to new cyber threats that previously did not represent a significant risk.

Unlike IT systems, where confidentiality of information is the priority, in OT the primary concern is the availability and integrity of processes. Disruption of an industrial control system can lead to serious operational failures, with economic and security repercussions. In addition, many OT devices and systems were designed decades ago without considering cybersecurity, meaning they continue to operate with outdated technologies, without security patches and with insecure communication protocols.

Attacks on industrial infrastructure have been on the rise in recent years, with notable incidents demonstrating the destructive potential of a security breach in these environments. Cases such as Stuxnet, the malware that affected nuclear centrifuges in Iran, or the attack on Ukraine's power grid in 2015, have highlighted the vulnerability of industrial systems and the urgent need to strengthen their defences. Threats can come from cybercriminal groups, nation-states, malicious employees or even human error that leaves critical networks exposed.

To address these challenges, it is necessary to adopt a comprehensive approach to cybersecurity in OT, combining technical measures with good organizational practices. Implementing controls such as network segmentation, strong authentication, continuous monitoring of systems, and updating software and firmware can significantly reduce risks. Likewise, awareness and training of operators and technicians is essential to detect and respond to potential security incidents before they become major problems.

International standards and regulations, such as the IEC 62443 series, the NIST cybersecurity framework, and the Cybersecurity and Infrastructure Security Agency (CISA) guidelines, provide robust frameworks for improving security in industrial environments. Adopting these standards enables organizations to develop effective protection strategies, aligned with industry best practices and regulatory requirements in different countries.

Another key aspect is the integration of cybersecurity into the lifecycle of industrial systems. As organizations modernize their infrastructure, it is crucial that security is considered by design and not as an afterthought. Implementing security architectures such as the defense-in-depth model, which combines multiple layers of protection, helps mitigate the impact of potential attacks and ensures a more effective response to incidents.

The future of OT cybersecurity is closely tied to the evolution of threats and the development of new technologies. With the advancement of artificial intelligence and machine learning, anomaly detection capabilities in industrial systems can be improved. However, attackers are also adopting more sophisticated tools, making OT cybersecurity a constantly evolving field.

Industrial organizations must recognize that cybersecurity is no longer an optional aspect, but a strategic necessity for the continuity of their operations. Protecting OT systems requires ongoing commitment, investment in technology and trained personnel, as well as a security culture that involves all levels of the company. Cyber resilience in industrial environments depends not only on the implementation of advanced technologies, but also on a comprehensive vision that allows risks to be anticipated and mitigated before they become crises.

Differences between IT and OT in Security

Security in technology environments has evolved over time to respond to the challenges and threats affecting both information technology (IT) and operational technology (OT) systems. Although both worlds share certain basic cybersecurity principles, their objectives, priorities and approaches are different due to the nature of the systems they protect. While IT security focuses on the protection of data, networks and computer systems, OT security is oriented towards ensuring operational continuity, physical security and the reliability of industrial processes.

One of the most fundamental aspects that differentiates IT from OT is the priority of security in each environment. In IT, confidentiality is the guiding principle, meaning that protecting information from unauthorized access is a major concern. In OT, on the other hand, priority falls on the availability and integrity of systems. The disruption of an industrial control system can lead to disastrous consequences, from the paralysis of a production plant to accidents with impact on human life or the environment.

System lifecycles also differ significantly. In IT, hardware and software are often updated frequently, with refresh cycles every few years. Applications and operating systems receive regular updates, and security patches are deployed on a regular basis. In OT, however, systems are designed to operate for decades without significant change. Many industrial infrastructures still rely on legacy technology that was not designed to address modern cyber threats, making it difficult to apply patches and upgrades without impacting operational continuity.

The IT security approach is based on the implementation of tools such as antivirus, firewalls, intrusion detection systems and data encryption to protect information against attacks. In OT, these mechanisms may not be viable due to the sensitivity of industrial devices and the need to minimize any impact on production processes. In many cases, security solutions used in IT can generate unacceptable latencies in OT or even cause failures in equipment that was not designed to support them.

Another key factor that differentiates IT from OT is the way networks are managed. IT networks are typically designed with an architecture based on connectivity and interoperability, allowing efficient communication between multiple systems and devices. In OT, network segmentation is critical to limiting access to industrial control systems and reducing the risk of cyber threat propagation. Many industrial networks operate with specific protocols that are not supported by IT standards, making it difficult to implement traditional security measures.

Access to systems also differs considerably between the two environments. In IT, users access networks and applications through centralized authentication and credentials, with access controls based on roles and privileges. In OT, access to control systems is often more restricted and, in many cases, is physically controlled, through terminals connected directly to the equipment. Credential management and access monitoring in OT can be more complex due to the existence of devices without modern authentication interfaces.

The threats and risks faced by IT and OT also differ. In IT, attacks are typically aimed at data exfiltration, credential theft, or service disruption through distributed denial of service (DDoS) attacks. In OT, attacks can have direct physical impacts, such as tampering with industrial processes, damaging machinery, or altering critical parameters in sensitive infrastructures such as power plants, transportation systems, or water distribution networks.

Incidents in OT can be harder to detect due to the limited visibility many organizations have into their industrial systems. While advanced monitoring and threat analysis tools exist in IT, in OT, anomaly detection relies heavily on manual monitoring and the knowledge of operational staff. Implementing real-time security solutions in industrial environments is challenging due to the diversity of devices and protocols in use.

The approach to incident response also varies between IT and OT. In IT, when a threat is detected, administrators can isolate the affected system, apply patches, and restore data from backups. In OT, such actions may not be feasible without disrupting production, requiring mitigation strategies to minimize operational impact. In some cases, the only option is to contain the threat without affecting the operation until a safe intervention can be planned.

Despite these differences, convergence between IT and OT is advancing rapidly due to industrial digitalization and the adoption of technologies such as the Industrial Internet of Things (IIoT) and cloud computing. This integration brings benefits in terms of efficiency and optimization, but also introduces new security risks that must be addressed with specialized strategies. Collaboration between IT and OT teams is essential to develop a security approach that respects the particularities of each environment without compromising the operation or protection of industrial assets.

Understanding the differences between IT and OT in security is essential to design effective cybersecurity strategies in industrial environments. Each sector has its own challenges and priorities, so it is necessary to adopt differentiated approaches that balance the protection of systems with the need to maintain operational continuity. The evolution of threats and increasing digitalization make OT security a constantly changing field, where adaptation and the implementation of good practices are key to guaranteeing the resilience of critical infrastructures.

Main Threats in Industrial Environments

Cybersecurity in industrial environments faces increasing challenges due to digitalization, interconnectivity, and the evolution of cyber threats. Industrial infrastructures rely on control systems that were designed to operate in closed and isolated environments, but convergence with information technology networks and the adoption of emerging technologies have exposed these infrastructures to new vulnerabilities. Threats in these environments can not only compromise data security, but can also affect the operability of systems, generate economic losses, and put the physical safety of workers and society at risk.

One of the most significant risks in industry is malware specifically designed to attack industrial control systems. Examples such as Stuxnet, Industroyer and Triton have shown that attackers can develop malicious programs capable of infiltrating critical infrastructure and manipulating industrial processes. These attacks can lead to the alteration of operating parameters, damage to sensitive equipment or even the destruction of key infrastructure. The problem is exacerbated when industrial systems rely on legacy software without security updates, making them easy targets for attackers.

Ransomware is another growing threat in the industrial arena. This type of attack encrypts files and systems, demanding a ransom in exchange for restoring access. In IT environments, the impact may be limited to data loss or temporary unavailability of services. However, in OT, ransomware can halt entire production lines, paralyze logistics operations, or affect power and water distribution. The inability to access control systems can lead to multimillion-dollar losses and critical operational risks. Many industrial organizations have fallen victim to this type of attack, forcing them to make difficult decisions about paying ransoms or rebuilding their systems.

Denial of Service (DoS) and Distributed Denial of Service (DDoS) attacks also pose a significant problem for industrial infrastructures. These attacks seek to saturate networks and systems with malicious traffic, preventing legitimate devices from operating normally. In the industrial context, a DDoS attack can affect communication between control systems and field devices, disrupting the monitoring and control of critical processes. The reliance on secure communication networks makes these attacks particularly dangerous in sectors such as energy, transportation, and manufacturing.

Tampering with sensors and control devices is another type of threat with potentially serious consequences. Industrial systems rely on sensors to monitor variables such as temperature, pressure, speed, and liquid levels. An attacker who is able to alter the readings of these sensors can fool operators and cause inappropriate responses in control systems. This can lead to mechanical failures, explosions, chemical spills, or power outages. Tampering with these devices can occur through unauthorized remote access or through physical attacks within industrial facilities.

Industrial espionage is also a growing concern in industrial cybersecurity. Companies and governments have fallen victim to targeted attacks aimed at stealing sensitive information about processes, designs, and proprietary technologies. Unlike other types of threats, industrial espionage is often highly stealthy and difficult to detect, as attackers seek to remain within systems for long periods of time without being discovered. Global competition has led certain state actors and cybercriminal groups to develop advanced tactics to infiltrate industrial networks and obtain strategic information without leaving obvious traces.

Internal risk is another factor that cannot be ignored. Not all threats come from external actors; many times, employees or contractors themselves can pose a danger to industrial security. Whether due to negligence, human error, or malicious actions, internal incidents can seriously compromise the security of systems. A worker connecting an infected device to the network, an operator misconfiguring a control system, or a disgruntled employee with privileged access can all create critical vulnerabilities that can be exploited by external attackers.

Lack of segmentation in industrial networks is another common problem that facilitates the spread of attacks. In many industrial facilities, control systems still share infrastructure with corporate IT networks without adequate security barriers. This means that an attack targeting the office network can spill over into production systems and directly impact plant operations. Lack of segmentation allows an attacker who gains access to a non-critical entry point to move laterally to reach the most sensitive systems in the infrastructure.

Supply chain vulnerabilities have also increased risk in industrial environments. Many organizations rely on third-party vendors for equipment maintenance, software provision, and system management. If one of these vendors is compromised, attackers can use their legitimate access to infiltrate industrial networks. These types of attacks have been used to introduce malware in software updates, compromise devices before delivery, or exploit third-party access credentials. Reliance on third-party vendors without adequate security controls poses a significant risk to the integrity of industrial systems.

Advances in artificial intelligence and machine learning have given rise to new threats in industrial cybersecurity. Attackers can use advanced algorithms to automate attacks, evade detection systems, and adapt their strategies in real time. At the same time, AI is also being used in defense, allowing anomalous patterns in industrial networks to be detected and incidents to be responded to more efficiently. However, the balance between attack and defense in this area continues to evolve, and organizations must stay up to date to avoid being at a disadvantage against attackers.

Threats in industrial environments continue to increase in sophistication and frequency, requiring organizations to take proactive measures to protect their critical infrastructure. The combination of targeted attacks, technological vulnerabilities and internal risks makes industrial cybersecurity a complex challenge that requires specialized strategies. Maintaining a robust security posture is not only a matter of protecting data, but of ensuring the continuity of operations that are critical to the economy and the security of society.

Cybersecurity OT Standards and Regulations

Cybersecurity in operational technology has become a global priority due to the increasing digitalization of industrial infrastructures and the constant evolution of cyber threats. As industrial control systems become integrated with information technology networks and connected to the Internet, the need to establish specific regulations and standards for the protection of these environments has become indispensable. Governments, international organizations and industrial sectors have developed regulatory frameworks to ensure the security of critical infrastructures and minimize the risks associated with cyber attacks.

One of the main regulatory frameworks in OT cybersecurity is the IEC 62443 series of standards, developed by the International Electrotechnical Commission. This standard provides a comprehensive approach to the protection of industrial control systems, defining specific requirements for manufacturers, integrators and infrastructure operators. IEC 62443 establishes principles of defense in depth, access management and network segmentation, offering a set of best practices adapted to the reality of industrial environments. Its adoption allows organizations to strengthen their security posture and reduce the attack surface on their systems.

In the United States, the National Institute of Standards and Technology (NIST) has developed the NIST Cybersecurity Framework (CSF) for critical infrastructure. This framework provides guidelines for identifying, protecting, detecting, responding to, and recovering from security incidents in OT environments. Its flexibility makes it applicable to different industrial sectors, allowing organizations to adapt their security strategies to their specific needs. In addition, NIST has published the SP 800-82 guide, which focuses on protecting industrial control systems and applying best practices to reduce security risks in these environments.

In the European Union, the Network and Information Security Directive (NIS2) establishes mandatory requirements for the cybersecurity of operators of essential services and providers of critical infrastructure. This regulation obliges industrial companies to implement advanced security measures, report cyber incidents and ensure the resilience of their operations. With the entry into force of NIS2, organizations must reinforce their security strategies and comply with stricter standards in risk management and the protection of OT systems.

Another relevant framework is the ISO/IEC 27001 standard, which, although more focused on information security management in IT environments, can also be applied in OT. This standard establishes a security management system based on risk identification, implementation of controls and continuous improvement. By adopting ISO 27001 in industrial environments, companies can establish structured security policies and ensure compliance with international regulations.

In the energy sector, the NERC CIP (North American Electric Reliability Corporation Critical Infrastructure Protection) regulations establish specific standards for the protection of electrical infrastructure in North America. These regulations impose strict security requirements for electric grid operators, including access controls, system monitoring and incident response. Complying with NERC CIP is essential to ensure the stability and security of the electrical supply, minimizing the impact of potential cyberattacks on energy infrastructure.

In the industrial arena, compliance with regulations such as the Network and Information Systems Security Regulation in China, the Critical Infrastructure Protection Act in Germany, and the Industrial Cybersecurity Regulation in Singapore demonstrates the growing global concern for the protection of OT systems. Each country has developed specific regulations according to its needs and industrial contexts, establishing legal frameworks that oblige organizations to implement security controls and report cyber incidents.

The adoption of OT cybersecurity regulations not only responds to the need to protect critical infrastructures, but also to the growing pressure from governments and customers to ensure the security of industrial environments. Companies that do not comply with these regulations can face legal sanctions, loss of contracts and damage to their reputation. Implementing a compliance-based approach allows organizations to reduce risks and strengthen their position in the global market.

One of the challenges in implementing OT cybersecurity regulations is the diversity of industrial systems and the coexistence of technologies from different generations. Many industrial infrastructures operate with equipment that was designed decades ago, without considering modern security requirements. Adapting these systems to current regulations can be complex, especially when security updates can affect the stability of production processes. To address this challenge, organizations must adopt risk mitigation strategies that balance security with operational continuity.

Another key aspect in implementing OT cybersecurity regulations is the need for staff training and awareness. Meeting security standards not only involves the adoption of advanced technologies and tools, but also the training of operators, engineers and administrators in good cybersecurity practices. Creating a security culture within organizations is essential to ensure that regulations are effectively enforced and human errors that can lead to vulnerabilities in systems are minimized.

Compliance audits and assessments are critical to ensuring the effectiveness of OT cybersecurity regulations. Many regulations require companies to conduct regular reviews of their security controls, identify potential gaps, and take corrective action. Audits can be conducted by regulatory bodies, specialized consultancies, or internal security teams. Maintaining a continuous assessment program allows organizations to adapt to new threats and ensure that their systems meet the security requirements required by current regulations.

OT cybersecurity regulations continue to evolve in response to the increasing sophistication of cyberattacks and the development of new technologies. As threats become more advanced, governments and international bodies are constantly updating their regulations to address emerging challenges in industrial environments. Organizations must keep up with these changes by adopting dynamic security strategies that enable them to comply with legal requirements and protect their critical infrastructures from cyber risks.

Security Models for Critical Infrastructures

Critical infrastructure plays a fundamental role in the stability of modern societies, as it includes essential sectors such as energy, transportation, telecommunications, healthcare, and water supply. Due to their strategic importance, these infrastructures have become attractive targets for malicious actors looking to cause massive disruptions, create chaos, or even affect national security. Protecting these systems requires the implementation of specific security models that mitigate risks and ensure operational continuity in the face of potential cyber and physical threats.

One of the most widely used approaches to protecting critical infrastructure is the defense-in-depth model. This concept is based on the implementation of multiple layers of security to prevent an attacker from compromising the system with a single point of failure. Defense-in-depth combines physical, technical and administrative controls, ensuring that even if one layer of security is breached, other barriers exist to hinder the attacker's progress. In industrial environments, this model translates into network segmentation, strong authentication, constant monitoring and restricted access to critical systems.

The Zero Trust model has emerged as a key strategy for protecting critical infrastructure in an environment where interconnectivity and remote access have increased significantly. Unlike traditional approaches that assume threats come only from the outside, Zero Trust adopts the premise that no entity, whether internal or external, should be considered trusted by default. This model requires continuous verification of identities, enforcement of least privileges, and the use of microperimeter segmentation to limit access to industrial systems.

Another widely used model is the approach based on the NIST cybersecurity framework. This framework provides a flexible structure for organizations to identify, protect, detect, respond to, and recover their systems from security threats. Applied to critical infrastructures, it allows for risk assessment, the definition of security policies, and the implementation of appropriate controls to minimize the impact of potential incidents. Adopting this model facilitates the alignment of security strategies with international regulations and industry-recognized best practices.

The security model based on network segmentation is essential in critical infrastructures due to the need to isolate operating systems from corporate systems. The convergence of information technology and operational technology networks has increased the exposure of industrial systems to external threats, so network segmentation allows for the establishment of protective barriers between the different levels of the infrastructure. The application of this model involves the use of security zones, the implementation of industrial firewalls and the use of traffic control mechanisms to restrict communication between critical devices and external networks.

The proactive security approach relies on identifying and mitigating threats before they can cause damage to the infrastructure. Unlike reactive models, which rely on responding to incidents after they occur, proactive security uses threat analysis, real-time traffic monitoring, and artificial intelligence tools to anticipate potential attacks. In critical infrastructures, this model is especially useful for detecting anomalous patterns that may indicate attempts at intrusion or manipulation of control systems.

The risk management model has established itself as an essential methodology for the protection of critical infrastructures. This approach involves the identification of critical assets, the assessment of threats and vulnerabilities, and the implementation of controls proportional to the level of risk. In the industrial context, risk management allows organizations to prioritize resources and apply security measures based on the potential impact of each threat. This model is complemented by periodic audits and evaluations to ensure the effectiveness of protection strategies.

The cyber resilience model focuses on the ability of a critical infrastructure to withstand, respond to, and recover from security incidents. Since no system is completely immune to attacks, this approach seeks to minimize the impact of a cyberattack and ensure operational continuity through recovery plans, system redundancy, and incident response testing. Adopting this model in critical infrastructure ensures that operations can be quickly restored following a disruption, reducing downtime and associated financial losses.

The application of the continuous monitoring model has proven to be an effective strategy in protecting critical infrastructures. This approach relies on the constant monitoring of systems to detect anomalies and respond immediately to potential threats. Through the use of security operations centers (SOC) and intrusion detection systems, organizations can gain real-time visibility into security events and make informed decisions to mitigate risks. In critical infrastructures, where early detection of incidents is key to preventing disruptions, continuous monitoring is one of the most effective tools to reinforce security.

The security model based on the principle of least privilege is another essential approach in the protection of critical infrastructures. This model establishes that each user, system or process should only have the permissions necessary to perform its function, thus reducing the attack surface and limiting the impact of possible security compromises. In industrial environments, where multiple actors can interact with control systems, the implementation of strict access controls and identity management become key elements to reduce risks.

Critical infrastructures require a combination of security models to ensure they are protected against current and future threats. Integrating approaches such as defense in depth, Zero Trust, network segmentation and cyber resilience creates a secure and resilient environment against potential attacks. The constant evolution of threats makes security in critical infrastructure a dynamic challenge that requires continuous updating of security strategies, technologies and practices. Implementing appropriate models not only protects industrial systems, but also safeguards the well-being of society and the stability of strategic sectors.

Secure Architecture in OT Systems

Security in operational technology systems is a fundamental aspect for the protection of critical infrastructures, industrial plants and automation environments. Unlike information technology systems, OT systems require a security approach that guarantees operational continuity and minimizes interruptions. To achieve this, the implementation of a secure architecture is essential, allowing the reduction of risks associated with cyber attacks, configuration errors and unauthorized access.

The design of a secure architecture in OT systems is based on the principle of defense in depth, which seeks to establish multiple layers of security to make access to critical systems difficult. Network segmentation is one of the most important strategies in this approach, as it allows industrial systems to be isolated from corporate networks and limits the spread of threats. Through the implementation of security zones and the use of industrial firewalls, data traffic can be controlled and communications between devices at different levels can be restricted.

The implementation of operational technology networks must follow a structured model that prioritizes security. The Purdue reference architecture, widely used in industrial environments, defines a hierarchy of levels that segments systems into different layers, from the corporate network to field devices. This model allows for specific security controls to be established at each level, ensuring that only necessary communications are allowed between the different network segments. Respecting this architecture is essential to prevent direct access to control systems from external networks.

The use of firewalls specific to industrial environments is a key measure for the protection of OT systems. Unlike conventional firewalls, these devices are designed to work with industrial protocols and filter traffic based on rules specific to control systems. Implementing firewalls between security zones makes it possible to restrict communication between networks and prevent unauthorized access to critical systems. In addition, monitoring traffic in real time facilitates the detection of anomalies and possible intrusion attempts.

Access control is another fundamental pillar in a secure OT architecture. User and device authentication must be strict, avoiding the use of shared credentials and ensuring that only authorized personnel have access to industrial systems. Implementing multi-factor authentication adds an additional layer of protection, reducing the risk of unauthorized access even if a user's credentials are compromised. In addition, identity management must consider the principle of least privilege, ensuring that each user only has access to the functions necessary for their job.

Security in communication between industrial devices is a critical aspect in OT architecture. Many protocols used in industry were designed without considering cybersecurity, making them vulnerable to attacks such as data manipulation or information interception. Implementing encryption in communications and using secure protocols, such as OPC UA instead of older protocols, helps protect the integrity and confidentiality of data transmitted on the network.

Network segmentation by creating security zones is an effective strategy to minimize the risks of cyberattacks in industrial environments. Separating the control network from the corporate network and Internet access reduces exposure to external threats. Using demilitarized networks (DMZ) between the IT area and the OT area allows the transfer of information to be controlled without compromising the security of industrial systems. In addition, segmentation within the OT network itself prevents an attack on an individual component from affecting the entire system.

Continuous network monitoring is an essential practice to detect potential threats in real time. Implementing intrusion detection systems (IDS) and intrusion prevention systems (IPS) in OT networks allows for identifying suspicious activities and responding immediately to security incidents. These systems should be configured to analyze network traffic for anomalous patterns without interfering with the operation of industrial devices.

Patch and update management in OT systems is challenging due to the need to maintain operational stability. However, it is critical to mitigate vulnerabilities that can be exploited by attackers. Scheduling maintenance windows to apply security updates and implementing mitigation measures when certain systems cannot be updated can reduce the risk of exploitation of known flaws. Additionally, using application whitelists helps prevent unauthorized software from running on industrial devices.

The use of redundant architectures and incident recovery plans is key to ensuring the resilience of OT systems. The existence of backup systems and the ability to automatically failover minimise the impact of a cyber attack or technical problem on the operation of the infrastructure. Implementing regular backups and verifying their integrity ensures that system recovery is fast and effective in the event of a security incident.

Remote access to OT systems must be restricted and protected by advanced security mechanisms. Using virtual private networks (VPNs) with strong encryption and implementing secure access solutions such as remote access gateways reduce the risks associated with connecting third-party operators and vendors. Additionally, implementing audit logs to monitor remote user activities allows suspicious access to be detected and responded to in a timely manner.

Staff training is a key factor in the effectiveness of secure architecture in OT systems. Operators, engineers and administrators must be trained in good cybersecurity practices, threat identification and incident response procedures. Awareness of security risks and the adoption of strict control policies on the use of removable devices and media prevent malware infections and unauthorized access.

The constant evolution of threats makes it necessary for the secure architecture of OT systems to be reviewed and improved on an ongoing basis. Performing security audits, penetration tests and attack simulations allows vulnerabilities to be identified and infrastructure defenses to be strengthened. Implementing adaptive strategies and adopting advanced technologies ensure that security in OT systems remains effective in the face of the challenges of today's digital environment.

Risk Assessment in Operational Technology

Risk assessment in operational technology is an essential process to ensure the security and continuity of industrial systems. Unlike in information technology, where data protection is the priority, in OT risk assessment focuses on the availability, integrity and security of physical processes. Any disruption in an industrial environment can cause significant economic losses, damage to infrastructure and, in some cases, affect the safety of people.

The risk assessment process in OT begins with the identification of critical assets. This involves a detailed analysis of all devices, systems and networks that are part of the industrial infrastructure. Each asset must be catalogued according to its function, operational importance and level of criticality. Accurate identification of these elements allows organizations to understand which parts of the system require the most protection and how they can be affected by different threats.

Once assets have been identified, the next step is threat analysis. In an OT environment, threats can come from multiple sources, including cyberattacks, technical failures, human errors, and natural events. Targeted attacks on industrial infrastructure have increased in frequency and sophistication, so it is essential to consider threats such as specialized malware, unauthorized access, data manipulation, and internal sabotage. In addition, environmental factors such as fires, floods, or power failures must also be considered, as they can compromise the stability of operational systems.

Vulnerability analysis is another key component in risk assessment. Many industrial infrastructures operate on legacy systems that were designed without cybersecurity in mind. These systems may lack authentication mechanisms, use insecure communication protocols, or not receive regular security updates. Identifying these weaknesses is essential to determining which parts of the system can be exploited by attackers or affected by internal flaws. Conducting security audits, penetration testing, and attack simulations helps detect vulnerabilities before they can be used in a real incident.

Once the threats and vulnerabilities have been identified, the impact that each risk could have on the infrastructure is assessed. In OT environments, the impact of an incident is not limited to data loss or temporary service interruption, but can directly affect production, physical security and business stability. An attack that manipulates the operation of an industrial control system could lead to machine failures, explosions, spills of hazardous substances or even large-scale power outages. Assessing these impacts allows prioritizing the mitigation of the most critical risks.

Risk calculation is based on the combination of the probability of an incident occurring and its potential impact. Risk assessment models typically use quantitative or qualitative scales to rank each risk and determine what level of response is required. Some frameworks, such as the NIST risk analysis model, IEC 62443, or ISO 31000, provide structured methodologies for performing this calculation and establishing appropriate mitigation plans.

A fundamental part of risk assessment in OT is the implementation of security controls that reduce the probability of an incident occurring or minimize its effects if it does materialize. Network segmentation, traffic monitoring, strong authentication, and the implementation of intrusion detection mechanisms are some of the strategies that can strengthen security in industrial systems. In addition, the application of security patches and software updates are essential measures to eliminate known vulnerabilities and improve the resistance of systems to cyberattacks.

Risk management in OT is not a static process, but must be continually reviewed and updated. As new threats emerge and changes are introduced to the infrastructure, risks need to be reassessed and mitigation strategies adjusted. Conducting regular audits and updating incident response plans ensures that the organization is prepared to deal with any eventuality.

The human factor plays a crucial role in risk assessment in OT. Operators and technicians of industrial systems must be trained to identify threats, respond appropriately to security incidents, and follow established security protocols. Lack of awareness or incorrect application of security measures can make employees a vulnerable point within the infrastructure. Implementing training programs and incident simulations helps reinforce the security culture within the organization.

Real-time monitoring is a powerful tool to improve risk assessment in OT. Through monitoring systems, it is possible to detect anomalous patterns in the operation of industrial systems and proactively respond to potential threats. Technologies such as artificial intelligence and machine learning are being used to analyze large volumes of data in real time and anticipate failures or attacks before they have a significant impact on the infrastructure.

Regulatory compliance is another important aspect of risk management in OT. Many industries are subject to regulations that establish mandatory security requirements for the protection of critical infrastructure. Complying with regulations such as NERC CIP, NIS2 or IEC 62443 not only reduces operational risks, but also protects organizations from legal penalties and financial losses associated with non-compliance. Integrating risk assessment with regulatory requirements allows security strategies to be aligned with globally established best practices.

Risk assessment in operational technology is a continuous process that requires the participation of multiple actors within the organization. The combination of mitigation strategies, active monitoring, staff training and regulatory compliance allows to reduce exposure to threats and ensure the resilience of industrial infrastructures. As digitalization advances and threats evolve, risk management in OT becomes an increasingly complex task, but indispensable for the security and stability of industrial systems.

Implementing Security Controls in OT

Security in operational technology requires the application of specific controls that protect industrial systems against cyber threats and ensure operational continuity. Unlike information technology environments, where security is oriented towards the protection of data and computer systems, in OT the main objective is to ensure the availability and reliability of industrial processes. The implementation of security controls in these environments must consider the nature of the systems, their operational restrictions, and compatibility with legacy technologies that are still in operation.

The first step in implementing security controls in OT is network segmentation, a fundamental strategy to minimize the risk of attack propagation. The Purdue reference architecture establishes a layered segmentation model that allows industrial networks to be isolated from corporate networks and access to control systems to be delimited. By using industrial firewalls, access control lists, and the configuration of demilitarized networks, communication between critical areas can be restricted and unauthorized access from outside can be prevented.

Access control is another fundamental pillar in OT security. In many industrial environments, control systems have traditionally been operated without strong authentication mechanisms, which represents a significant vulnerability. Implementing multi-factor authentication for users and adopting identity control mechanisms help restrict access to authorized personnel only. Applying the principle of least privilege ensures that each user only has access to the functions necessary to perform their job, reducing the possibility of misconfigurations or improper access.

Monitoring and supervising OT networks is essential for early detection of threats and traffic anomalies. Implementing intrusion detection systems can identify suspicious behavior patterns in industrial infrastructure and trigger alerts for anomalous events. Unlike IT environments, where detection systems can automatically block traffic, in OT any response needs to be carefully evaluated to avoid operational disruptions. Complementing monitoring with detailed access and audit logs facilitates incident investigation and identification of network vulnerabilities.

Using application whitelists is an effective strategy for protecting industrial control devices. Instead of relying on traditional antivirus solutions, which can cause interference in OT systems, whitelists allow only authorized software to run, blocking the installation and execution of unrecognized programs. This measure prevents the introduction of malware into control systems and reduces the risk of targeted attacks that exploit vulnerabilities in unauthorized software.

Protecting the integrity of data and communication between industrial devices is a key aspect in implementing security controls. Many protocols used in OT were designed without considering cybersecurity, making them vulnerable to interception and manipulation attacks. Adopting secure protocols and using encryption in communications helps prevent the alteration of critical data in control systems. Implementing measures such as digital signature on operation orders and using VPNs for remote connections improves the security of information transmitted on the network.

Remote access to control systems is a necessity in many industrial environments, but it also represents a significant risk if appropriate measures are not implemented. Limiting remote access to authorized personnel, using encrypted connections, and implementing continuous monitoring of remote sessions are key strategies to prevent unwanted access. Using secure gateways and implementing strong authentication for remote access reduces exposure to external threats and protects critical systems from uncontrolled access.

Patch and update management in OT environments presents unique challenges due to the need to ensure operational stability. Unlike IT environments, where updates can be applied more frequently, in OT the impact of each change needs to be assessed before it is implemented. Planning maintenance windows, performing testing in isolated environments, and implementing mitigation measures for systems that cannot be updated helps maintain a balance between security and operational continuity.

Staff training is a key factor in implementing security controls in OT. Lack of cybersecurity knowledge on the part of operators and technicians can become one of the main vulnerabilities within industrial infrastructure. Developing training programs that include security best practices, threat awareness, and incident response protocols helps strengthen the organization's security posture. Conducting simulation exercises and periodically assessing staff knowledge levels helps identify areas for improvement and reinforce the security culture.

Developing incident response plans is an essential part of the OT security strategy. No system is completely immune to attacks, so having established procedures for incident detection, containment and recovery is essential to minimise their impact. Defining roles and responsibilities within the response team, establishing effective communication channels and carrying out response simulations can improve the ability to react to any threat that compromises the security of industrial systems.

Regulatory compliance is another key aspect of implementing security controls in OT. Complying with standards such as IEC 62443, NERC CIP, and the NIST Cybersecurity Framework not only helps reduce risks but also ensures that the organization is aligned with international best practices. Integrating regular audits and continuous assessment of security controls ensures that industrial infrastructure remains protected against evolving threats.

Implementing security controls in OT requires a structured approach that balances system protection with the need to ensure operational continuity. Combining network segmentation, access control, continuous monitoring, patch management and staff training can reduce the attack surface and improve the resilience of industrial infrastructure. The constant evolution of threats makes security in OT environments a dynamic process that must be continuously reviewed and updated to meet emerging challenges.

Security in SCADA and Industrial Control Systems

Industrial control systems play a fundamental role in the operation of critical infrastructures and industrial processes, allowing the monitoring and control of machinery, production plants and distribution networks. Within these systems, SCADA (Supervisory Control and Data Acquisition) platforms are widely used to collect real-time data and manage equipment distributed across large geographical areas. The increasing digitalisation and connectivity of these systems has significantly increased their exposure to cyber threats, making it essential to implement specific security strategies to protect their integrity and operational continuity.

SCADA systems were originally designed to operate in isolated environments, with no connection to external networks or exposure to cyber threats. However, the evolution of technology and the need for interconnectivity have led to their integration with corporate networks and cloud platforms. This convergence has opened the door to new risks, as any vulnerability in the IT network can be exploited to access industrial control systems. Attackers can exploit these weaknesses to disrupt operations, manipulate industrial processes, or even cause physical damage to the infrastructure.

One of the main challenges in SCADA security is the lack of security updates and patches in many industrial systems. Because these environments operate with high availability and cannot afford frequent outages, software updates are often postponed or ignored. This leaves systems exposed to known vulnerabilities that can be exploited by malicious actors. Implementing a patch management strategy should consider operational constraints, planning updates during maintenance periods and applying mitigation measures when it is not possible to update software immediately.

Access control is a critical aspect of SCADA and industrial control system security. Many facilities still use default credentials or weak authentication schemes, which facilitate unauthorized access to systems. Implementing multi-factor authentication and identity management policies can reduce the risk of unauthorized access. Additionally, applying the principle of least privilege ensures that each user only has access to the functions necessary for their job, minimizing the impact if an account is compromised.

Network segmentation is one of the most effective strategies for protecting SCADA systems. Separating the control network from the corporate network and Internet access reduces the attack surface and limits the ability of attackers to move laterally within the infrastructure. The use of industrial firewalls, access control lists, and demilitarized networks allows security barriers to be established between different network segments, ensuring that only legitimate communications are allowed between critical systems.

Continuous monitoring of SCADA systems is a fundamental practice for early threat detection. Implementing intrusion detection systems and behavioral analysis tools allows you to identify anomalies in network traffic and respond quickly to suspicious activity. Collecting event logs and security audits helps maintain a history of access and operations, facilitating incident investigation and continuous improvement of security strategies.

Remote access to SCADA systems must be managed with extreme care, as it represents one of the main attack avenues in industrial environments. Limiting remote access to authorized personnel only and using encrypted connections through VPNs or secure gateways helps reduce the associated risks. In addition, implementing monitoring and logging mechanisms for remote sessions allows any unusual activity to be detected and immediate responses to potential threats can be made.

Application whitelisting is an effective technique to prevent the execution of malicious software on industrial control systems. Unlike traditional antivirus, which can cause interference in OT environments, whitelisting allows only previously authorized programs to run, blocking any attempt to install unrecognized software. This strategy helps protect SCADA systems against malware and targeted attacks that attempt to introduce malicious code into control devices.

Securing communication protocols is a key aspect of SCADA security. Many industrial protocols were designed without considering cybersecurity, making them vulnerable to data interception and manipulation attacks. Encrypting communications and using secure protocols can prevent attackers from altering critical information or injecting malicious commands into control systems. In addition, validating data integrity through digital signatures reduces the risk of manipulation of operational information.

The human factor is one of the main vulnerabilities in the security of SCADA and industrial control systems. Training staff in good security practices, threat awareness, and incident response procedures is essential to strengthen the organization's security posture. Conducting cyberattack simulations and response tests helps prepare operators and technicians to act effectively in the event of a real threat.

Regulatory compliance is a key aspect in protecting SCADA and industrial systems. Complying with standards such as IEC 62443, NERC CIP, and the NIST Cybersecurity Framework ensures that organizations adopt best practices in industrial security. Conducting security audits and periodically assessing implemented controls allows for identifying areas for improvement and adjusting protection strategies based on evolving threats.

Operational resilience in SCADA systems must be a priority within the security strategy. Implementing redundancy in critical systems, establishing incident recovery plans and performing regular backup testing ensures that the infrastructure can withstand and recover quickly from a cyber attack or technical failure. Operational continuity in industrial environments depends on the ability of SCADA systems to operate safely even under adverse conditions.

Security in SCADA and industrial control systems is a complex challenge that requires a comprehensive approach. The combination of network segmentation, access control, continuous monitoring, communications protection and staff training can significantly reduce the risks associated with cyberattacks and ensure the stability of critical infrastructures. As threats evolve, it is essential for organizations to adopt dynamic strategies and constantly review their security measures to keep their SCADA systems protected against the challenges of the digital environment.

Protection of Industrial Networks

Industrial networks are the fundamental pillar of operational technology and enable communication between control systems, automation devices and central servers that monitor and execute critical processes. The increasing digitalization of industrial infrastructures has brought with it multiple benefits in terms of efficiency and productivity, but it has also increased the attack surface, exposing networks to new cyber threats. Protecting industrial networks has become a priority to ensure operational continuity and system security, preventing interruptions, data manipulation and unauthorized access.

One of the most important principles in protecting industrial networks is segmentation, which allows the infrastructure to be divided into distinct security zones to minimize the spread of attacks. Segmentation based on the Purdue reference model is a widely used strategy to structure networks into different security levels, separating the corporate network from the control network and isolating critical systems from potential external threats. The implementation of industrial firewalls and access control lists helps enforce this segmentation, ensuring that only legitimate communications are allowed between specific zones of the network.

Intrusion monitoring and detection are key components in an industrial network protection strategy. Implementing intrusion detection systems can identify anomalous traffic patterns that could indicate an attempted attack or unauthorized access. Unlike in IT environments, where detection systems can automatically block suspicious traffic, in industrial networks it is crucial to perform a careful assessment before taking any action that could affect operability. Continuous traffic monitoring and event log collection facilitate early threat identification and enable a quick and efficient response to security incidents.

Network access control is another critical aspect of securing industrial infrastructure. Many industrial networks still allow unauthenticated connections or use default credentials that can be easily exploited by attackers. Implementing multi-factor authentication and centralized identity management helps reduce the risk of unauthorized access. Additionally, applying the principle of least privilege ensures that each user only has access to the parts of the network necessary to perform their job, minimizing the exposure of critical systems.

Protection against external threats is not enough if industrial networks do not have adequate mechanisms to detect and mitigate internal threats. The use of role-based access solutions and the implementation of detailed activity logs make it possible to identify unusual behavior within the network. Internal attacks can be the result of human error, misconfigurations, or even malicious actions by employees with privileged access. Monitoring and auditing network access is an essential measure to prevent security incidents generated from within the organization.

Using device whitelists is an effective strategy to limit network connectivity to only authorized equipment. In many industrial environments, third-party devices and uncontrolled equipment can introduce security risks if not managed properly. Implementing controls based on MAC addresses or digital certificates allows you to restrict connectivity to only approved devices, thereby reducing the possibility of unauthorized access or the introduction of malware into the network.

Data encryption in transit is a key measure for protecting information circulating in industrial networks. Many industrial protocols were designed without security in mind, making them vulnerable to interception and manipulation attacks. Adopting secure protocols and implementing encryption in communications helps prevent attacks such as man-in-the-middle attacks, which allow attackers to alter data transmitted between control devices. Authentication and validation of messages using digital signatures is another strategy that reinforces the integrity of communication in the network.

Vulnerability management in industrial networks is a constant challenge due to the presence of legacy systems that may not have security updates. Proactive identification of vulnerabilities through security audits and assessments allows flaws to be detected before they can be exploited by attackers. Application of patches and software updates must be carefully planned to minimise the impact on operability, and where updating certain devices is not possible, compensating controls must be implemented to mitigate the associated risks.

Remote access to industrial networks is an operational necessity in many infrastructures, but it also represents one of the biggest threats if not managed correctly. Using virtual private networks with strong encryption and implementing secure gateways can protect remote connections and prevent unauthorized access. In addition, establishing remote access sessions with monitoring and audit logs makes it easier to identify suspicious activities and reduces the risk of control system manipulation.

Redundancy and resilience strategies are essential to ensure the availability of industrial networks in the event of attacks or technical failures. The implementation of redundant network architectures and the adoption of automatic failover mechanisms allow operational continuity to be maintained in the event of any interruption. Backups of network configurations and periodic validation of their integrity ensure that, in the event of an attack or failure, systems can be restored quickly and safely.

Staff training is a key factor in protecting industrial networks. Operators, engineers and administrators must be trained in good cybersecurity practices, threat identification and incident response. Lack of knowledge about OT security can lead to vulnerabilities within the infrastructure, so it is essential to develop ongoing training programs and simulation exercises that prepare staff to face cyberattacks.

Compliance with security regulations and standards strengthens the protection of industrial networks and ensures that organizations adopt best practices in cybersecurity. Complying with regulatory frameworks such as IEC 62443, NIST CSF and NERC CIP ensures that industrial infrastructure has adequate controls to mitigate risks and address emerging threats. Conducting security audits and periodically updating protection policies helps maintain a secure environment aligned with industry demands.

Securing industrial networks is an ongoing process that requires the implementation of multiple layers of security. Network segmentation, access control, intrusion detection, communications encryption, and vulnerability management are just a few of the essential strategies to reduce risks and strengthen infrastructure resilience. As threats evolve, it is imperative to maintain a dynamic approach to protecting industrial networks, ensuring that security measures are updated and adapted to the challenges of the ever-changing digital environment.

Access Management and Authentication in OT

Access management and authentication in operational technology are critical aspects of ensuring the security of industrial systems and the protection of critical infrastructure. Unlike IT environments, where access is typically well structured and controlled through centralized directories and multi-factor authentication, access management in OT has historically been less rigorous. Many industrial control systems were designed in an era where cybersecurity was not a central concern, leading to weak credentials, unauthenticated access, and default configurations that pose significant security risks.

One of the main challenges in access management in OT is the large number of devices and systems that require constant interaction from operators, maintenance technicians and external suppliers. In many industrial facilities, access to control systems still relies on shared credentials, default passwords or weak authentication mechanisms. This approach represents a critical vulnerability, as any attacker who manages to gain access to a compromised credential could operate the systems without restrictions, putting the integrity and availability of industrial processes at risk.

To mitigate these risks, multi-factor authentication has emerged as one of the most effective strategies for protecting OT systems. Combining factors such as passwords, smart cards, biometric authentication or physical tokens significantly reduces the likelihood of unauthorized access. In environments where physical security is a key component, implementing biometric authentication for access to control rooms or critical terminals allows for an additional layer of protection to be added, ensuring that only authorized personnel can interact with the systems.

The principle of least privilege is another fundamental pillar of access management in OT. Each user, system or device should have only the permissions necessary to perform its specific function. Limiting privileges prevents an attacker with compromised access from making unauthorized changes to critical systems. Role-based privilege segmentation allows users to be classified into different access levels based on their responsibilities, reducing the exposure of control interfaces to people who do not require access to certain sensitive functions.

Using centralized identity management solutions is a key strategy for controlling and auditing access in OT. Implementing an authentication directory that manages user credentials allows security policies to be applied uniformly across the entire infrastructure. In addition, these solutions facilitate the revocation of access when an employee leaves the organization or changes roles, preventing old credentials from remaining active and being used in potential attacks. Integrating these systems with existing security controls allows for more efficient administration and better visibility into who has access to which systems at all times.

Access monitoring is an essential measure to detect intrusion attempts and quickly respond to any suspicious activity. Audit logs allow you to analyze access patterns, identify anomalies, and generate alerts for unusual behavior. Implementing user behavior analysis tools helps detect out-of-hours access, repeated failed authentication attempts, or lateral movements within the network that could indicate an attempt to compromise the system. Combining these mechanisms with artificial intelligence and machine learning allows for improved threat detection in real time.

Remote access represents one of the biggest threats to OT security if not managed properly. Many organizations allow remote connections for system monitoring or equipment maintenance by third-party vendors. However, a lack of proper controls on these accesses can open the door to attackers looking to exploit vulnerabilities in remote connections. Implementing virtual private networks with strong encryption, secure gateways, and multi-factor authentication reduces the risks associated with remote access. Additionally, establishing remote access sessions with monitoring and audit logs helps ensure that each connection is authorized and monitored in real time.

Physical access to control systems must also be managed with strict security measures. Restricting access to server rooms, control stations and critical devices prevents unauthorized persons from directly manipulating the systems. Combining electronic controls, such as access cards and biometric authentication, with traditional measures, such as surveillance and visitor control, strengthens protection against internal and external threats. In many critical infrastructures, implementing a layered security model allows for multiple control points to be established to prevent unauthorized access to the most sensitive areas.

Using temporary credentials and just-in-time access is an effective strategy to mitigate the risks associated with access management in OT. Instead of providing permanent access to contractors or vendors, solutions can be implemented that grant permissions temporarily and only for the time necessary to perform a specific task. Once the authorized period has ended, the credentials are automatically revoked, reducing the possibility of improper access in the future. This practice is especially useful in the maintenance of critical infrastructures where multiple external actors may require access at different times.

The human factor remains one of the main vulnerabilities in access management and authentication in OT. Training staff in good security practices, raising awareness of the risks of using weak credentials, and applying rigorous procedures in access management are essential to strengthening infrastructure security. Developing ongoing training programs and conducting attack simulations helps prepare operators to recognize phishing attempts and apply security measures effectively.

Access and authentication management in OT must be addressed with a comprehensive approach that combines advanced technologies with good operational practices. Implementing multi-factor authentication, privilege segmentation, access monitoring, remote access control and physical access protection are key measures to reduce risks and ensure the security of industrial systems. As threats evolve, it is necessary to maintain a dynamic strategy that allows for continuous updating and improvement of control mechanisms, ensuring that only authorized personnel have access to the organization's critical systems.

Segmentation and Security Zones in Critical Infrastructures

Network segmentation and the implementation of security zones are essential elements for the protection of critical infrastructures. These environments include sectors such as energy, transport, healthcare and industry, where operational continuity is essential and any interruption can generate serious economic and social consequences. The growing connectivity between operational technology systems and information technology has increased the attack surface, making it essential to adopt security strategies that limit the spread of threats and minimise the impact in the event of cyber incidents.

One of the most widely used models for segmenting critical infrastructures is the Purdue architecture, which establishes a structured hierarchy to divide systems into different security levels. This architecture separates the network into layers ranging from corporate systems to field devices, ensuring that control systems have no direct exposure to external networks. Tiered segmentation allows for security barriers to be established that prevent attackers from moving laterally within the infrastructure, reducing the risk that an incident in one part of the network will compromise the entire operation.

The establishment of security zones within a critical infrastructure allows for the definition of protection perimeters based on the level of risk and the criticality of the assets. These zones are created with the aim of restricting access between network segments and applying differentiated controls based on the sensitivity of the information and the processes involved. One of the most common strategies is the implementation of demilitarized networks (DMZ), which act as intermediaries between the corporate network and the control network. Secure access servers and systems that require interaction with external networks are located in this zone, but without directly compromising industrial systems.

Controlling traffic between different security zones is a key aspect of network segmentation. Implementing industrial firewalls allows for filtering and restricting connections between segments, ensuring that only authorized devices and services can communicate with each other. Additionally, the use of access control lists reinforces security by defining specific rules on who can access which systems and under what conditions. Deep packet inspection in firewalls allows malicious traffic attempts or unauthorized access to be identified before they can affect the infrastructure.

Isolation of critical networks is another key strategy within infrastructure segmentation. In many cases, it is recommended that industrial control systems operate on networks completely separate from the corporate network to minimize the risk of attacks from IT environments. The existence of direct connections between these networks can be an entry point for attackers looking to exploit vulnerabilities in administrative systems and then move laterally into operational systems. Physical segmentation or the use of independent virtual networks can reduce these risks and ensure the integrity of control systems.

Segmentation in critical infrastructures should not only be applied at the network level, but also in access management. Implementing role-based controls and privilege segmentation ensures that each user only has access to the systems and functions necessary for their job. Adopting the principle of least privilege reduces the exposure of the most sensitive systems to users who do not require access to them, thus limiting the possibility of human error or improper access.

Traffic monitoring in different security zones is essential to detect intrusion attempts and respond to potential threats. Implementing intrusion detection and prevention systems allows for identifying anomalies in network traffic and alerting about suspicious activities. In critical infrastructures, where system availability is a priority, it is important that these solutions are configured so that they do not cause operational interruptions, but rather allow for a rapid and effective response to incidents.

Remote access to systems within critical infrastructures must be controlled through segmentation and robust authentication mechanisms. Implementing secure access gateways and encrypted virtual private networks can ensure that only authorized users can connect to control systems. In addition, monitoring remote sessions and implementing audit logs helps detect anomalous behavior and prevent unauthorized access.

Segmentation should also extend to the protection of network-connected field devices and sensors. With the proliferation of the Industrial Internet of Things, many industrial devices are exposed to networks with external connectivity, increasing the possibility of attacks. Segmenting these devices into dedicated networks and restricting their access to only authorized systems reduces the possibility of them being compromised and used as attack vectors against the rest of the infrastructure.

Compliance with cybersecurity regulations and standards is a key factor in implementing segmentation and security zones in critical infrastructure. Regulations such as IEC 62443, NERC CIP, and the NIST Cybersecurity Framework provide clear guidelines on network segmentation and the implementation of security controls in industrial systems. Conducting regular audits and penetration tests allows the effectiveness of segmentation strategies to be assessed and security measures to be adjusted based on emerging threats.

Effective segmentation of critical infrastructure requires a comprehensive approach that combines technical measures with organizational policies. Collaboration between operational technology and information technology teams is essential to design a network architecture that ensures security without affecting the operability of systems. Training staff on the importance of segmentation and the proper use of security zones reinforces the implementation of these strategies and minimizes the risks associated with human error or incorrect configurations.

The constant evolution of cyber threats makes segmentation and security zones in critical infrastructure a dynamic process that must be continually reviewed and updated. As industrial networks modernize and adopt new technologies, it is essential that segmentation strategies evolve in parallel to maintain system security. The combination of network segmentation, access control, continuous monitoring and regulatory compliance creates a secure and resilient environment that protects critical infrastructure from modern cybersecurity challenges.

Physical Security in Industrial Environments

Physical security in industrial environments is an essential component in protecting critical infrastructure and operational technology systems. Unlike in information technology environments, where security typically focuses on protecting data and networks, in industrial environments the integrity of physical assets is critical to ensuring operational continuity and the safety of people. The combination of external and internal threats requires a structured approach that integrates physical barriers, continuous monitoring, and strict access controls to prevent sabotage, theft, vandalism, or interference with production.

Unauthorized access to industrial facilities represents one of the main risks to physical security. In many plants, electrical substations and distribution centers, control systems are located in areas with restricted access, but without adequate security measures, leaving them exposed to tampering. To mitigate this risk, the implementation of access controls that restrict access to authorized personnel is essential. The use of proximity cards, biometric authentication and electronic locks ensures that only accredited employees can access sensitive areas. In addition, the integration of access logs with periodic audits helps detect anomalies and prevent incidents.

Video surveillance monitoring is one of the most effective strategies for reinforcing physical security in industrial environments. Installing cameras at strategic points allows for real-time monitoring of activities within facilities and the detection of suspicious behavior. Cameras with facial recognition and motion detection technology can generate automatic alerts when unauthorized access or unusual activities are identified. Integrating these systems with security control centers allows for rapid response to incidents and facilitates the collection of evidence in the event of a security event.

Perimeter protection is another key aspect of industrial physical security. Many critical infrastructures are located over large areas and require additional measures to prevent intrusions. Installing security fences with motion detection sensors, access barriers and perimeter lighting systems reduces the likelihood of unauthorized access. In environments where the risk of sabotage or theft is high, implementing security patrols and surveillance drones can strengthen area protection and deter potential threats.

Access control to critical equipment and devices is just as important as perimeter security. In many industrial facilities, control and monitoring systems are located in areas where multiple employees and vendors have access. To prevent tampering, security measures must be implemented to restrict physical access to these devices. Installing security cabinets with electronic locks, using security seals on sensitive terminals, and implementing audit controls ensure that only authorized personnel can operate or modify critical systems.

Insider risk is a latent threat in industrial environments. Not all vulnerabilities come from outside; in many cases, employees or contractors themselves can pose a danger to infrastructure security. Implementing role-based access control policies helps minimize the exposure of critical systems to unauthorized personnel. In addition, physical security training and awareness of the risks of unauthorized access or operational negligence help strengthen the security culture within the organization.

Protection against sabotage and physical attacks is a growing concern in industrial security. In sectors such as energy, transportation, and manufacturing, a targeted attack on a facility can lead to massive disruptions and significant economic losses. To prevent such incidents, it is essential to conduct physical vulnerability assessments and establish contingency plans. Simulating attack scenarios, implementing emergency response procedures, and redundancy in critical infrastructure can mitigate the impact of potential sabotage.

Safe storage of hazardous materials and sensitive equipment is another key element in industrial physical security. In facilities where flammable, chemical or radioactive substances are handled, it is essential to have strict protocols for their storage and handling. The implementation of segregated storage areas, the application of leak detection sensors and the training of personnel in handling hazardous materials help to reduce the associated risks. Likewise, the integration of fire extinguishing systems and emergency alarms reinforces the protection of facilities against possible incidents.

Remote access to industrial systems also poses a risk to physical security. While cybersecurity is critical to protecting remote connections, the physical security of the equipment used to access the industrial network must also be considered. Implementing secure workstations, using encrypted devices, and restricting access to USB ports and removable media prevent unauthorized manipulations that could compromise the integrity of the systems.

Maintaining security infrastructure is a critical aspect of physically protecting industrial environments. Many facilities have security systems in place that can become obsolete or fail to operate over time. Conducting regular inspections of fencing, surveillance cameras, access controls, and detection systems can identify weaknesses and make improvements before they are exploited by malicious actors. Constantly updating security protocols and modernizing the technologies used ensure that physical protection remains effective in the face of new threats.

Compliance with physical security regulations in industrial environments is essential to ensure the protection of infrastructure and the safety of personnel. Standards such as ISO 27001, IEC 62443 and national regulations establish guidelines on the implementation of physical controls in critical facilities. Conducting compliance audits and adopting security best practices allows organizations to stay aligned with regulatory requirements and strengthen the resilience of their infrastructures against potential threats.

Physical security in industrial environments is an essential component of a comprehensive strategy for protecting critical infrastructure. The combination of access controls, continuous monitoring, perimeter protection and internal risk management makes it possible to minimise threats and ensure the operational continuity of industrial systems. The constant evolution of risks requires a continuous review and improvement of security strategies, ensuring that infrastructures remain protected against any type of threat, whether physical or cyber.

Cybersecurity in Industry 4.0

Digital transformation has given rise to Industry 4.0, a new era in manufacturing and industrial production characterized by interconnectivity, advanced automation, and the use of emerging technologies such as the Industrial Internet of Things, artificial intelligence, real-time data analytics, and cloud computing. While these advancements have significantly improved operational efficiency and data-driven decision making, they have also introduced new cybersecurity challenges. The convergence between operational technology and information technology has increased the attack surface, exposing industrial infrastructures to cyber threats that previously did not pose a significant risk.

One of the main challenges in Industry 4.0 cybersecurity is the proliferation of connected devices. Sensors, robots, distributed control systems and data management platforms are now interconnected in networks that, in many cases, have access to the Internet or cloud platforms. The lack of adequate security controls on these devices can allow attackers to exploit vulnerabilities and gain unauthorized access to production systems. Many of these technologies use communication protocols designed without considering cybersecurity, facilitating attacks such as data interception, command manipulation and malicious code execution in critical environments.

The use of the cloud in Industry 4.0 has raised new concerns regarding data privacy and integrity. Companies are increasingly relying on cloud-based platforms to store and process large volumes of industrial information, which implies additional risks if adequate security measures are not implemented. Protecting data in transit and at rest, robust authentication and continuous access monitoring are key aspects to mitigate the risks associated with cloud computing. In addition, the reliance on third-party providers for infrastructure management poses additional challenges in risk management and industrial data sovereignty.

Artificial intelligence and machine learning have improved the efficiency of industrial processes, but they have also opened the door to new attack vectors. AI-based systems rely on training data that can be manipulated by attackers to alter their behavior. Threats such as model manipulation, malicious data injection, and evasion of AI-based detection systems represent emerging challenges in Industry 4.0 cybersecurity. Implementing data validation mechanisms and continuous auditing of AI algorithms are critical to ensuring the reliability of these systems in industrial environments.

The convergence of information technology and operational technology has made industrial infrastructures more vulnerable to targeted attacks. As production systems increasingly rely on connected networks and integration with digital platforms, attackers can exploit vulnerabilities in the corporate network to infiltrate control systems. Network segmentation and the adoption of security architectures based on the Zero Trust model can minimize these risks by restricting access and continuously verifying the identity and intent of each connection within the industrial network.

Ransomware has emerged as one of the top threats in Industry 4.0. Attackers have identified industrial infrastructures as lucrative targets due to the impact that a disruption in production can have on the supply chain. A ransomware attack on a manufacturing plant can paralyze operations, affect the supply of essential products, and result in millions in losses. Implementing segmented backups, segmenting networks, and restricting access to control systems reduces the likelihood of a ransomware attack spreading in an industrial environment.

Remote access to industrial systems is an operational necessity in Industry 4.0, but it also represents a significant attack vector if not managed correctly. Using virtual private networks with strong encryption, multi-factor authentication, and restricting remote access to only those devices and users strictly necessary are essential strategies to minimize risks. In addition, continuous monitoring of remote sessions and implementing audit logs allow for the rapid detection and response to suspicious activity on production systems.

Supply chain security is a critical aspect in Industry 4.0. Many companies rely on third-party vendors for the provision of software, hardware, and maintenance services, which introduces additional risks if these vendors do not meet adequate cybersecurity standards. Supply chain attacks have increased in frequency, with attackers seeking to compromise software or devices prior to delivery to infiltrate industrial infrastructures. Evaluating suppliers, implementing security controls in contracts, and continuously auditing the supply chain are critical practices to mitigate these risks.

The human factor remains one of the biggest vulnerabilities in Industry 4.0 cybersecurity. Training staff in good security practices, raising awareness of threats such as phishing and social engineering, and adopting strict policies in credential and access management are key measures to reduce the risk of security incidents. Implementing ongoing training programs and simulating cyberattacks can improve staff's ability to respond to potential threats.

Compliance with cybersecurity regulations and standards in Industry 4.0 is essential to ensure the protection of critical infrastructure and the security of industrial data. Regulations such as IEC 62443, NIST CSF and the NIS2 Directive establish specific guidelines for the protection of industrial control systems and risk management in connected environments. Adopting these regulations and conducting security audits allows organizations to identify vulnerabilities and improve their defense strategies against cyberattacks.

The evolution of Industry 4.0 has brought significant benefits in terms of automation and efficiency, but it has also increased the complexity of cybersecurity in industrial environments. The combination of advanced technologies, increasing interconnectivity and dependence on the cloud requires a comprehensive approach that combines technical measures, risk management and staff training. Organizations that implement cybersecurity strategies adapted to the challenges of Industry 4.0 will be better prepared to protect their infrastructures, minimize risks and ensure operational continuity in an increasingly digitalized environment.

Forensic Analysis in OT Incidents

Operational technology forensics is a fundamental discipline for the investigation of security incidents in industrial environments. As critical infrastructures and industrial control systems have been subject to increasingly sophisticated attacks, it is essential to have methodologies and tools that allow identifying the root cause of incidents, assessing the impact and strengthening defenses to prevent future attacks. Unlike information technology environments, where forensic analysis focuses on data recovery and identifying security breaches in conventional systems, in OT the focus must consider operational continuity, process integrity and the interaction between physical and digital devices.

One of the main challenges in forensic analysis of OT incidents is the diversity of systems and protocols used in the industry. Many infrastructures operate with devices designed decades ago, which do not have advanced logging or monitoring capabilities. In addition, industrial control systems use proprietary protocols that make it difficult to collect digital evidence using traditional forensic analysis tools. To address this challenge, it is essential to implement monitoring and data capture strategies adapted to industrial environments, allowing the collection of relevant information without affecting the stability of critical systems.

The first step in a forensic analysis of OT incidents is the preservation of evidence. Any alteration to records, devices or systems can compromise the investigation and make it difficult to identify the cause of the incident. To prevent the loss of critical information, procedures must be in place for the secure capture and storage of event logs, configuration files and network traffic. Disk cloning, memory imaging and extracting logs from control systems are essential practices to ensure the integrity of the evidence.

Identifying the attack entry point is a key aspect in forensic investigation of OT incidents. Attackers can exploit vulnerabilities in control devices, insecure remote access, or even configuration errors to infiltrate the infrastructure. By analyzing access logs, correlating events, and inspecting network traffic, it is possible to reconstruct the sequence of events that led to the system compromise. In OT environments, where availability is a priority, this process must be carried out without interrupting the operation of control systems, using analysis techniques in isolated environments or redundant systems.

Analyzing attacker behavior helps you understand the techniques used and assess the impact of the incident on the infrastructure. In many cases, attackers seek to remain within the system for long periods before executing destructive actions or extracting sensitive information. Identifying patterns of lateral movement, changes in configurations, and manipulation of control devices helps determine the magnitude of the attack and the possible intentions behind it. In the case of attacks targeting critical infrastructure, this analysis can provide valuable information to strengthen security and prevent similar attacks in the future.

Event reconstruction is a crucial phase in the forensic analysis of OT incidents. By correlating logs from different devices, monitoring systems and industrial sensors, it is possible to establish a detailed timeline of the attack. This process requires the use of specialized tools that allow interpreting data from multiple sources and visualizing the progression of the incident. In many cases, attackers try to erase traces of their activity, so identifying indicators of compromise and comparing historical logs can be key to detecting evidence tampering.

Incident response in OT environments must balance the need to investigate the attack with the operational continuity of the infrastructure. Unlike IT environments, where it is possible to isolate a compromised system without significantly affecting the operation, in OT any disruption can lead to serious consequences for production or the safety of people. For this reason, forensic analysis in OT must be part of a well-structured incident response plan, which includes specific protocols for collecting evidence without compromising system stability.

Learning from security incidents is one of the key benefits of OT forensics. Each attack provides valuable insights into existing vulnerabilities, attacker tactics, and gaps in security controls. Documenting the findings and implementing corrective measures helps strengthen an organization's security posture and reduce the likelihood of future attacks. Additionally, sharing information with other organizations and industrial cybersecurity communities helps improve collective protection against emerging threats.

The use of artificial intelligence and machine learning in OT forensics has made it possible to improve the detection of anomalies and the identification of attack patterns in real time. These technologies can analyze large volumes of data efficiently, facilitating the identification of suspicious events and the correlation of information between different systems. However, the application of these tools in industrial environments must be carefully evaluated to avoid false positives and ensure that they do not interfere with the normal operation of control systems.

The human factor remains a critical element in the forensic analysis of OT incidents. Training staff in identifying and responding to security incidents is essential to ensure an effective investigation. Operators and technicians must be prepared to recognize signs of malicious activity, report suspicious events, and collaborate with security teams in collecting evidence. Conducting incident response simulations and exercises helps improve reaction capacity and strengthens the security culture within the organization.

Compliance with cybersecurity regulations and standards in OT is a key aspect of forensic incident management. Regulations such as IEC 62443, NIST 800-82, and NERC CIP establish specific requirements for incident response and evidence collection in industrial environments. Complying with these regulations not only helps improve infrastructure security, but also facilitates collaboration with regulatory entities and security agencies in the event of incidents affecting critical infrastructure.

Forensic analysis of OT incidents requires a specialized approach that considers the particularities of industrial systems, the need for operational continuity, and the diversity of threats to which critical infrastructures are exposed. Combining evidence collection strategies, attacker behavior analysis, real-time monitoring, and staff training can improve incident response capabilities and strengthen the resilience of industrial environments against increasingly sophisticated cyberattacks.

Industrial Cybersecurity Incident Response

Cybersecurity incidents in industrial environments represent a growing threat to operational continuity, system integrity and the security of critical infrastructure. The digitalisation of industrial processes and the convergence between information technology and operational technology have increased the exposure of control systems to cyberattacks. Incident response in these environments must be meticulous and structured, as any disruption can have significant impacts on production, personnel safety and the provision of essential services.

Preparation is a key element in responding to industrial cybersecurity incidents. Before an attack occurs, organizations must have a response plan in place that establishes clear procedures, roles, and responsibilities for personnel tasked with managing the crisis. Lack of a defined protocol can lead to delays in identifying the incident and increase the impact of the attack. An effective plan should include measures for early threat detection, attack containment, system recovery, and post-incident learning.

Detecting incidents in industrial environments is challenging due to the diversity of devices and systems that make up the infrastructure. Attackers can exploit vulnerabilities in control networks, field devices, or remote access systems without being immediately detected. Real-time monitoring tools, intrusion detection systems, and network traffic behavior analysis are essential to improve detection capabilities. Correlating events between different systems makes it possible to identify anomalies that could indicate the presence of a threat before it causes significant damage.

Once an incident has been identified, the next step in response is containment to prevent the attack from spreading and compromising other systems. In information technology environments, containment measures may include disconnecting affected equipment or blocking suspicious IP addresses. However, in operational technology, isolating a system without proper assessment can impact production and introduce additional risks. Network segmentation and implementing strict access controls facilitate containment without the need to completely shut down operations.

Attack eradication is a critical phase that requires identifying the source of the threat and removing any traces of the attacker from systems. Depending on the type of attack, it may be necessary to perform forensic analysis on compromised devices, restore security settings, and apply software patches to fix exploited vulnerabilities. In some cases, attackers may have installed backdoors to maintain access to the system even after initial containment. Thorough log review and application whitelisting help detect and eliminate potential attacker persistence.

Recovery of industrial systems affected by an incident must be carried out with caution to avoid secondary damage. In IT environments, restoring backups can be a quick solution to recover compromised systems, but in OT, restoration must be planned so as not to affect the operability of control devices. Validating data integrity and performing functionality tests before reactivating systems are critical steps in safe recovery. In cases where systems have been altered by an attack, it may be necessary to restore configurations to their original state and reinforce security controls before resuming normal operation.

Effective communication during an industrial cybersecurity incident is crucial to coordinate the response and mitigate the impact of the attack. Within the organization, security, operations, and management teams must be aligned on the response strategy. In addition, it is important to establish communication protocols with external suppliers, regulatory authorities, and other stakeholders in case the incident affects critical infrastructure on which third parties depend. Transparency and speed in communication help reduce uncertainty and improve the ability to react to the crisis.

Post-incident analysis is an essential phase to improve the organization's resilience to future threats. Once the crisis has been contained and systems restored, a detailed assessment of the attack should be conducted to identify which security flaws allowed the system to be compromised. Documenting the incident, the actions taken, and the lessons learned facilitates continuous improvement in cybersecurity strategies. Updating the incident response plan based on these learnings ensures that the organization is better prepared to face similar attacks in the future.

Staff training plays a key role in the effective response to industrial cybersecurity incidents. Operators, engineers and system administrators must be trained in identifying warning signs, response procedures and preventive measures they can take to reduce risks. Conducting attack simulation exercises can test the reaction capacity of security teams and detect areas for improvement in the response strategy.

Regulatory compliance is an important aspect of incident response in industrial environments. Many regulations require organizations to report security incidents and take corrective action to prevent future attacks. Standards such as IEC 62443, NERC CIP, and the NIST Cybersecurity Framework set out specific guidelines on how to manage incidents in critical infrastructure. Ensuring compliance with these standards not only helps improve the security of the organization, but also facilitates cooperation with government entities and other industry players in managing cyber threats.

The evolution of industrial cybersecurity threats requires organizations to adopt a proactive approach to incident response. The implementation of artificial intelligence and predictive analysis tools makes it possible to anticipate attacks and improve the early detection of anomalies. Collaboration between different industrial sectors and the sharing of information on emerging threats strengthens the capacity for collective defense against attacks targeting critical infrastructure.

Industrial cybersecurity incident response should be a structured and dynamic process that reduces the impact of attacks, restores system operability, and strengthens the organization's security posture. The combination of preparation, early detection, containment, eradication, recovery, and post-incident analysis is essential to mitigate risks and ensure the resilience of industrial environments in an ever-evolving threat landscape.

Common Malware and Attacks in OT

Operational technology systems have historically been designed to operate in isolated environments, with a focus on the stability and availability of industrial processes. However, with increasing digitalization and interconnectivity between industrial systems and information technology networks, cyberattacks targeting critical infrastructure have increased significantly. The introduction of malware into OT systems can compromise not only the operation of a plant or facility, but also the safety of workers and the stability of strategic sectors such as energy, transportation, and manufacturing.

One of the most well-known types of malware to have affected OT systems is Stuxnet, a computer worm that was specifically designed to sabotage industrial control systems. Stuxnet managed to infect thousands of devices worldwide and demonstrated that cyberattacks could cause physical damage to critical infrastructure. Its sophistication lay in its ability to modify the operation of programmable logic controllers without being detected, allowing industrial processes to be manipulated stealthily. This type of attack set a precedent in OT security, highlighting the vulnerability of industrial systems to threats specifically designed to disrupt their operations.

Another malware designed to target industrial infrastructure is Industroyer, used in cyberattacks against power grids. This malware had the ability to communicate directly with industrial protocols used in power distribution systems, allowing attackers to disconnect power stations and cause blackouts. Its modular structure allowed it to adapt to different industrial environments and execute commands directly on control systems. Industroyer showed that attackers can manipulate OT devices without needing to affect conventional IT systems, making protecting these environments even more challenging.

Triton is another example of malware targeting OT systems, but with a focus on industrial safety systems. This malicious code was designed to compromise safety controllers used in chemical and power processing plants, with the intention of disabling protective mechanisms and generating dangerous conditions within the facilities. Triton's ability to modify the logic of safety controllers makes it one of the most dangerous threats to industrial cybersecurity, as it could lead to incidents with catastrophic consequences.

In addition to malware designed specifically for OT, many industrial infrastructures have been affected by ransomware, a type of malicious software that encrypts files and systems, demanding payment to regain access. Ransomware attacks such as WannaCry and Ryuk have affected manufacturing plants, transportation companies, and hospitals, causing significant disruption to their operations. In OT environments, where availability is a priority, a ransomware attack can force critical processes to stop, which can result in millions of dollars in losses and damage to infrastructure.

Denial of service attacks also pose a significant threat to OT systems. This type of attack seeks to flood a network or system with malicious traffic, preventing legitimate devices from being able to communicate with each other. In an industrial infrastructure, such an attack can affect communication between control systems and field devices, leading to operational failures and reducing the ability of operators to monitor and manage processes. The lack of availability of real-time monitoring systems can delay response to critical events, increasing security risks and impacting production.

Manipulation of sensors and control devices is another tactic used by attackers to affect OT systems. Many industrial infrastructures rely on sensors to measure variables such as temperature, pressure, and material flow. If an attacker manages to alter the readings of these sensors, control systems can respond inappropriately, leading to production failures or even dangerous situations. In sectors such as the chemical industry and power generation, this type of attack can lead to explosions, spills of hazardous substances, or massive blackouts.

Supply chain attacks have become one of the most commonly used tactics by cybercriminals to infiltrate OT environments. In many cases, attackers compromise a vendor's software or hardware before it reaches the industrial infrastructure. In this way, malicious code or vulnerabilities are inadvertently introduced into the organization's network, allowing attackers access without the need to exploit traditional security flaws. This type of attack has proven to be highly effective, as many organizations rely on external vendors to update and maintain their control systems.

Social engineering attacks have also been used to compromise OT systems. Attackers often take advantage of the lack of cybersecurity awareness of some operators and employees to obtain access credentials or install malware on the network. Tactics such as phishing have proven effective in industrial environments, as many users are not trained to identify malicious emails or fraudulent links. Once attackers gain access to a privileged account, they can move around the network and compromise critical systems undetected.

To mitigate these risks, it is essential that organizations adopt security strategies tailored to OT environments. Network segmentation is one of the most effective measures to prevent malware from spreading within industrial infrastructure. Implementing industrial firewalls and restricting access between different levels of the network hinders attackers' mobility and reduces the attack surface.

Real-time monitoring is another key tool for detecting attacks on OT systems. Implementing intrusion detection systems and analyzing network traffic allows for identifying anomalous patterns and responding immediately to any compromise attempts. In industrial environments, where availability is a priority, it is essential to have tools that allow for early detection of threats without generating interruptions in operations.

Strengthening supply chain security and training staff in good cybersecurity practices are also essential elements to reduce the impact of attacks on OT. Validating suppliers and implementing strict controls on the installation of updates and new devices minimize the risk of malicious code being introduced into the network. Continuous staff training in threat identification and incident response improves organizations' ability to defend against attacks targeting their industrial systems.

Attacks in OT environments have evolved in sophistication and frequency, forcing organizations to rethink their security strategies. The combination of advanced malware, targeted attack techniques, and the increasing interconnectivity of industrial systems make cybersecurity in OT an increasingly complex challenge. Implementing adequate protection measures, constant monitoring, and staff training are fundamental aspects to ensure the security and resilience of industrial infrastructures against cyber threats.

Implementation of Firewalls and IDS/IPS in Industrial Networks

Industrial networks have evolved significantly with the convergence between operational technology and information technology, which has brought great benefits in terms of efficiency, real-time monitoring and process automation. However, this interconnectivity has increased the risk of cyber attacks, making it necessary to use specific protection tools, such as firewalls and intrusion detection and prevention systems. These mechanisms allow traffic to be filtered, suspicious activities to be detected and threats to be mitigated in real time, minimising the impact of a possible attack on industrial control systems.

Implementing firewalls in industrial networks is one of the most effective strategies to establish security barriers between different infrastructure segments. A firewall acts as a filter that controls network traffic based on predefined rules, allowing only authorized connections and blocking any unauthorized access attempts. In OT environments, proper firewall configuration is crucial, as excessive restriction can affect communication between critical systems, while overly permissive configuration can leave the infrastructure exposed to external or internal attacks.

There are different types of firewalls that can be implemented in industrial networks, depending on the level of security required and the complexity of the infrastructure. Packet filtering firewalls operate by inspecting each data packet based on its IP address, port, and protocol, allowing or denying its passage according to established rules. While this type of firewall is efficient at blocking unauthorized traffic, it does not offer protection against more advanced threats that can exploit vulnerabilities in industrial protocols.

Stateful inspection firewalls offer an additional layer of security by analyzing not only individual packets, but also the context of established connections. This type of firewall keeps track of active sessions and allows traffic to be filtered based on the state of connections, making it difficult for attacks that attempt to exploit communication between devices. In industrial networks, where stability is a priority, this approach allows legitimate data to continue to flow while blocking suspicious access.

Deep application firewalls, also known as next-generation firewalls, are the most advanced and offer additional capabilities such as packet content analysis, threat detection, and integration with threat intelligence systems. In OT environments, these firewalls can be configured to recognize specific industrial protocols and block malicious commands targeting control devices. This is especially useful for preventing targeted attacks that seek to disrupt industrial processes through manipulation of SCADA systems or programmable logic controllers.

Network segmentation using firewalls is a fundamental practice in industrial cybersecurity. Dividing the infrastructure into security zones with differentiated access levels allows critical systems to be isolated from less secure networks, such as the corporate network or remote access for suppliers. Implementing demilitarized networks between the IT network and the OT network facilitates monitoring and filtering traffic without compromising the integrity of industrial systems. In addition, the use of internal firewalls within the OT network can prevent the spread of threats in the event that a device is compromised.

Along with firewalls, intrusion detection systems (IDS) and intrusion prevention systems (IPS) are key tools for protecting industrial networks. An IDS monitors network traffic for suspicious activity and generates alerts when it detects anomalous patterns that could indicate an attack in progress. Unlike a firewall, which simply blocks or allows traffic based on predefined rules, an IDS analyzes traffic behavior and uses known threat signatures or anomaly detection algorithms to identify potential attacks.

The use of IDS systems in industrial networks allows for the detection of unauthorized access attempts, the presence of malware in the infrastructure, and activities that could indicate the manipulation of control systems. The configuration of these systems must consider the nature of the industrial operation, since an excess of false alerts can generate an additional burden on security teams and make it difficult to identify real threats. The combination of signature-based detection with behavior-based detection allows for more accurate analysis and reduces the possibility of false positives.

Intrusion prevention systems (IPS) take detection a step further by not only alerting on suspicious activity but also taking action to block attacks in real time. An IPS can stop malicious connections, isolate compromised devices, and apply dynamic rules to mitigate the impact of an attack without manual intervention. In OT networks, where availability is critical, IPS deployment should be done with caution to avoid disruption of legitimate industrial processes. Setting an IPS to passive monitoring mode before enabling automatic blocking allows you to assess its impact on the infrastructure and fine-tune your security rules.

Deploying firewalls, IDS and IPS in industrial networks requires careful integration with other security systems to maximize their effectiveness. Correlating events between these systems and network monitoring tools allows for a more complete view of activity across the infrastructure, facilitating threat identification and rapid incident response. Implementing audit logs and periodically reviewing security rules ensures that these systems remain up-to-date in the face of new threats and changes in network architecture.

Remote access is one of the areas where firewalls, IDS and IPS can play a critical role in protecting industrial networks. Attacks targeting remote connections have increased with the digitalization of industrial processes, and attackers seek to exploit vulnerabilities in access protocols or compromised credentials to infiltrate the OT network. Configuring firewalls to restrict remote access, along with implementing IDS to monitor external connection traffic and applying IPS to block intrusion attempts, significantly minimizes the risk of attacks coming from outside.

The combination of firewalls, IDS and IPS in industrial networks strengthens the security posture of the infrastructure and reduces exposure to cyber threats. Network segmentation, deep traffic inspection, anomaly detection and automatic incident response are key elements in a defense-in-depth strategy. The correct implementation and maintenance of these systems ensures the operational continuity of industrial processes and protects control systems against cyber attacks in an increasingly interconnected environment.

Using Zero Trust in Operational Technology

The Zero Trust security model has emerged as an effective approach to protecting critical infrastructure and industrial environments in an ever-evolving cyberthreat landscape. Unlike traditional perimeter-based security models, where users and devices within the network are assumed to be trusted, Zero Trust is based on the principle that no access should be trusted by default, regardless of its location. In operational technology, where system availability and integrity are paramount, implementing Zero Trust significantly reduces the risks associated with unauthorized access, lateral attacker movement, and infrastructure vulnerabilities.

One of the main challenges in applying Zero Trust in operational technology is the diversity of devices and systems that are part of industrial networks. Many devices in OT environments were designed without considering cybersecurity, operate with legacy software, and use communication protocols that lack authentication and encryption. Despite these limitations, the adoption of Zero Trust in OT can be achieved through network segmentation, strong authentication, and continuous monitoring of traffic and access. Implementing these principles allows for the establishment of protective barriers that make it difficult to exploit vulnerabilities and gain unauthorized access to critical systems.

Identity-based access control is a fundamental pillar of Zero Trust in OT. Instead of granting privileges based on a device's location within the network, each access must be verified based on the user's identity, device type, and connection context. Multi-factor authentication becomes an essential requirement to ensure that only legitimate users can interact with industrial control systems. Furthermore, applying the principle of least privilege ensures that each user and device has access only to the resources strictly necessary for its function, reducing the possibility of lateral movement in the event of a security compromise.

Network segmentation is another key strategy in implementing Zero Trust in industrial environments. In a traditional model, control and monitoring systems are typically connected in flat networks, allowing any device on the same network to freely communicate with other systems. This represents a significant risk, as an attacker who manages to compromise a single device can move laterally and access critical systems without restrictions. Zero Trust requires strict segmentation of the infrastructure through micro-segmentation, establishing policies that limit communication between devices and restricting traffic to only what is strictly necessary for operation.

Continuous monitoring and anomaly detection are essential elements for the effective implementation of Zero Trust in OT. Since this model does not assume trust in any user or device, it is essential to have monitoring systems that analyze network traffic, identify unusual patterns, and generate real-time alerts for potential security incidents. The use of behavioral analysis tools makes it possible to detect anomalous access or attempts to exploit vulnerabilities before they can compromise the infrastructure. In addition, the integration of artificial intelligence in these systems facilitates the identification of emerging threats and the automation of incident responses.

Remote access to OT systems is one of the most critical attack vectors in industrial infrastructures. In many cases, external vendors and maintenance technicians require remote access to devices and control systems, exposing the network to intrusion risks if not managed properly. Zero Trust enforces the principle of continuous verification, where each remote access session must be authenticated and monitored at all times. Implementing secure gateways, using encrypted tunnels, and real-time monitoring of remote sessions can mitigate the risk of unauthorized access and ensure the integrity of industrial systems.

The application of Zero Trust in OT also involves the adoption of data protection mechanisms and communications encryption. Many devices in industrial environments exchange critical information without any form of encryption, which facilitates data interception and manipulation attacks. Implementing end-to-end encryption in communications and using digital signatures for command validation make it possible to strengthen the security of the infrastructure and prevent alterations in control processes. In addition, protecting data at rest through encryption ensures that sensitive information remains secure even if an attacker manages to compromise a device.

Regulatory compliance is a key factor in the adoption of Zero Trust in operational technology. Standards such as IEC 62443 and the NIST Cybersecurity Framework establish principles aligned with Zero Trust, promoting the implementation of strict access controls, network segmentation, and continuous monitoring of infrastructure. Ensuring compliance with these standards not only strengthens the organization's security posture, but also facilitates risk management and collaboration with regulatory entities and other industry players.

The human factor plays a fundamental role in the implementation of Zero Trust in OT. Training staff in good security practices, awareness of the risk of unauthorized access and the adoption of strict authentication policies are key aspects to ensure the success of the model. Resistance to change can be a challenge in industrial environments, where operational continuity is a priority, so it is necessary to implement progressive adoption strategies and provide specific training to facilitate the transition to a Zero Trust model without affecting the stability of the systems.

The adoption of Zero Trust in operational technology represents a paradigm shift in the protection of critical infrastructure and industrial systems. The elimination of the concept of implicit trust, strict network segmentation, continuous authentication and real-time monitoring can significantly reduce the risk of cyberattacks in OT environments. As threats evolve and interconnectivity in industry continues to grow, the implementation of Zero Trust becomes an imperative necessity to ensure the security and resilience of industrial operations in a digitalized world.

Secure Communication Protocols in OT

Secure communication in operational technology is a critical aspect to ensure the integrity, availability and confidentiality of data circulating in industrial networks. Unlike information technology environments, where security protocols have been widely adopted, many OT infrastructures still operate with legacy systems that use insecure protocols designed in an era when cybersecurity was not a priority. The increasing interconnectivity between industrial devices, remote access and the digitalization of processes have increased the need to adopt secure communication protocols that protect the infrastructure against cyberattacks and unauthorized access.

One of the main challenges in implementing secure protocols in OT is the coexistence of legacy devices with more modern technologies. Many industrial control systems still use unencrypted communication protocols, making them vulnerable to data interception and manipulation attacks. Attackers can exploit this lack of security to execute man-in-the-middle (MITM) attacks, in which they intercept and modify communication between devices without being detected. To mitigate these risks, it is essential to implement protocols that include authentication and robust encryption in data transmission.

The OPC UA (Open Platform Communications Unified Architecture) protocol is one of the most advanced standards in OT communications security. Designed to replace previous versions such as OPC DA and OPC Classic, this protocol incorporates authentication based on digital certificates, end-to-end encryption and access control mechanisms. The implementation of OPC UA ensures the integrity and confidentiality of information in SCADA systems, programmable logic controllers and other industrial devices. In addition, its ability to operate on different platforms makes it a versatile solution for industrial environments with heterogeneous architectures.

Another widely used protocol in OT environments is Modbus, which has been a key part of industrial automation for decades. However, the standard version of Modbus lacks security mechanisms, making it susceptible to spoofing attacks, data modification, and unauthorized access. To address these shortcomings, extensions such as Modbus TCP with TLS have been developed, which incorporates encryption and authentication using digital certificates. Adopting secure Modbus reduces the possibility of attackers altering commands sent to industrial devices, thereby protecting the operation of critical infrastructures.

DNP3 (Distributed Network Protocol 3) is another protocol widely used in automation systems, especially in the electrical industry and in water and gas distribution infrastructures. While DNP3 has been a reliable solution for communication in SCADA systems, its original version did not include advanced security measures. To mitigate this problem, DNP3 Secure Authentication was developed, an enhanced version that introduces authentication using public key cryptography and protection against replay attacks. The implementation of this version of the protocol allows for enhanced communication security in critical distribution networks.

The MQTT (Message Queuing Telemetry Transport) protocol has gained popularity in Industry 4.0 due to its efficiency in real-time data transmission. Although MQTT was designed for bandwidth-constrained and low-latency environments, its implementation without security measures can expose OT systems to data interception and manipulation. To ensure security in its use, it is recommended to adopt MQTT with TLS/SSL, which allows encrypting communications and authenticating devices connected to the network. In addition, permission management in MQTT brokers allows restricting data access based on the roles and needs of the connected systems.

Using Secure Shell (SSH) in OT is a best practice to secure remote access to industrial devices. SSH replaces insecure protocols such as Telnet and provides an encryption layer that protects credentials and commands sent between operators and control systems. Its implementation in OT environments ensures that remote connections are secure and cannot be intercepted or manipulated by attackers. However, it is critical that access keys are managed appropriately and that the use of default configurations that may compromise system security is avoided.

Network segmentation and the implementation of OT-specific firewalls complement the security of communication protocols. While the use of secure protocols minimizes the possibility of eavesdropping attacks, network segmentation prevents an attacker who gains access to a device from moving freely within the infrastructure. Implementing industrial firewalls that filter traffic based on specific protocols helps restrict unauthorized connections and ensure that only legitimate systems can communicate with each other.

Monitoring and detecting anomalies in OT communications is essential to identify potential attack attempts before they compromise the infrastructure. Implementing intrusion detection systems (IDS) tailored to industrial protocols allows network traffic to be analyzed and suspicious patterns to be detected. Integrating behavioral analysis tools helps identify attempts at data manipulation, unauthorized access, or changes to control device configurations.

Regulatory compliance plays a key role in the adoption of secure communication protocols in OT. Standards such as IEC 62443 establish guidelines on the protection of communications in industrial systems, promoting the adoption of encryption, authentication and network segmentation. Ensuring compliance with these regulations allows organizations to reduce their exposure to cyber threats and improve the resilience of their infrastructures.

Training staff in the use of secure protocols is a key factor in protecting OT communications. Lack of knowledge about the vulnerabilities associated with insecure protocols can lead to incorrect configurations that compromise the security of the infrastructure. Conducting training and implementing clear security policies can reduce the risks associated with human error and improve the security posture of the organization.

The evolution of cyber threats has highlighted the need to adopt secure communication protocols in OT environments. The transition from insecure protocols to modern standards with encryption, authentication and access control is essential to ensure data integrity and the protection of critical infrastructures. The combination of advanced technologies, network segmentation, real-time monitoring and staff training can reduce the risks associated with interconnectivity in industrial systems and strengthen the security of operational technology in a digitalized world.

Cybersecurity in Power Systems and Electrical Networks

Cybersecurity in power systems and electrical grids is a strategic challenge that directly impacts the stability and security of countries. The modernization of electrical infrastructures and the adoption of digital technologies have increased operational efficiency, but have also exposed these systems to new cyber threats. Today's electrical grids rely heavily on industrial control systems, smart sensors, and remote communication, which increases the attack surface and requires the implementation of advanced security measures to mitigate risks.

Cyberattacks targeting electricity infrastructure have shown that these networks are vulnerable and that a well-planned intrusion can cause massive blackouts, interruptions in supply and damage to critical equipment. Cases such as the attack on the Ukrainian electricity grid in 2015 showed how attackers can access distribution systems and manipulate control equipment to cause widespread failures. Such incidents have raised awareness of the importance of cybersecurity in the energy sector and have prompted the adoption of specific regulations and standards for the protection of these infrastructures.

One of the main risks in electrical networks is the interconnectivity of industrial control systems with information technology networks. The integration of SCADA (Supervisory Control and Data Acquisition) systems with corporate networks allows for more efficient supervision, but also introduces vulnerabilities if adequate controls are not implemented. Network segmentation is one of the most effective strategies to minimize these risks, preventing attackers from accessing control systems through less secure networks. The implementation of demilitarized networks (DMZ) between IT and OT systems allows critical infrastructures to be isolated and exposure to external threats to be reduced.

Remote access is another critical factor in power grid cybersecurity. Many operators and service providers require access to control systems to perform maintenance and adjustments on the infrastructure. However, the use of weak credentials or the lack of multi-factor authentication can make it easier for attackers to access these systems. Implementing secure gateways, using VPNs with strong encryption, and real-time monitoring of remote sessions are essential measures to reduce the risk of unauthorized access.

Malware designed to attack electrical infrastructure is a constantly evolving threat. Examples such as Industroyer have shown that attackers can develop malicious software capable of directly communicating with industrial protocols used in power distribution networks. This type of malware can disable substations, manipulate operating parameters, and generate cascading failures that affect wide geographic areas. Implementing OT-specific intrusion detection systems and deep inspection of network traffic can help identify attack patterns before they cause significant damage.

Field device tampering is another major threat in power grids. Remote sensors, switches, and controllers can be compromised by attackers looking to disrupt power flow or create grid instability. Protecting these devices through strong authentication, communications encryption, and continuous monitoring is critical to ensuring infrastructure integrity. Additionally, implementing application whitelists on these devices can restrict unauthorized software from running, reducing the risk of being compromised through targeted attacks.

Ransomware has begun to pose a growing threat to energy sector companies. Such an attack can encrypt critical files in monitoring and control systems, affecting operators' ability to manage power flow and respond to incidents. Network segmentation, implementing segmented backups, and restricting access with minimum privileges are key strategies to minimize the impact of such attacks on electrical infrastructures.

Real-time monitoring is one of the most effective tools for improving cybersecurity in power grids. The implementation of behavioral analysis systems allows the detection of anomalies in the operation of the grid and the generation of alerts before a threat can materialize. The correlation of events between different levels of the infrastructure allows security teams to identify attack patterns and respond more effectively to possible incidents.

Regulatory compliance is a critical factor in cybersecurity in the power sector. Regulations such as NERC CIP in North America and the NIS2 Directive in Europe set strict requirements for the protection of critical energy infrastructure. These regulations require the implementation of access controls, network segmentation, threat monitoring, and incident response plans. Ensuring compliance with these standards not only improves infrastructure security, but also minimizes the possibility of regulatory penalties and financial losses resulting from cyberattacks.

Resilience of electricity networks against cyberattacks requires a combination of technical and operational strategies. Implementing redundancies in the infrastructure makes it possible to guarantee continuity of supply even if part of the network is compromised. The ability to recover from incidents also depends on the preparation of staff, so cybersecurity training and the implementation of attack simulations are essential to improve emergency response capacity.

Strengthening cybersecurity in electricity networks is an ongoing process that requires adaptation to new threats and modernization of existing infrastructures. The adoption of advanced technologies such as artificial intelligence and machine learning allows for improved threat detection and automated responses to incidents in real time. Collaboration between energy sector companies, government agencies and cybersecurity experts is key to strengthening the protection of these infrastructures and ensuring the stability of the electricity supply in an increasingly digitalized environment.

Protecting Manufacturing Plants from Cyberattacks

Manufacturing plants have evolved with the incorporation of advanced technologies such as automation, robotics, and the interconnectivity of devices in industrial networks. Digitalization has improved efficiency and productivity, but it has also exposed these environments to new cyber threats. A cyber attack targeting a manufacturing plant can impact production, compromise product quality, and result in significant economic losses. Protecting these environments requires a comprehensive strategy that combines technical, operational, and organizational measures to mitigate the risks associated with cyber attacks.

One of the main risks in modern manufacturing is the convergence between operational technology systems and information technology. The integration of industrial control systems with cloud platforms and corporate networks facilitates remote management and process optimization, but also increases the attack surface. Attackers can exploit vulnerabilities in IT networks to gain access to OT systems, manipulate production devices or disrupt plant operations. Network segmentation is one of the most effective measures to reduce this risk, establishing barriers between the corporate network and industrial control systems using firewalls and differentiated security zones.

Remote access is another critical point in manufacturing plant cybersecurity. Many organizations allow suppliers and technicians to access industrial equipment remotely to perform maintenance and updates. Without proper controls, these accesses can become a gateway for attackers looking to compromise the infrastructure. Implementing secure gateways, multi-factor authentication, and remote session monitoring helps reduce the risk of unauthorized access. Additionally, restricting remote connections to specific periods only and logging all activities performed improves traceability and incident response.

Malware represents one of the most dangerous threats to manufacturing plants. Ransomware, in particular, has affected multiple companies in the sector, paralyzing production lines and demanding payments for the recovery of systems. An attack of this type can spread quickly through industrial networks if adequate containment measures are not implemented. Network segmentation, the use of application whitelists, and restricting access with minimum privileges help limit the spread of malware in the event of an infection. In addition, implementing backups on isolated systems ensures data recovery without relying on paying ransoms to attackers.

Denial of service attacks can impact the availability of industrial control systems in a manufacturing plant. This type of attack can disrupt communication between sensors, programmable logic controllers, and SCADA systems, directly impacting production. Protection against these types of threats requires the implementation of industrial firewalls configured to filter suspicious traffic, limiting network access from unknown IP addresses, and real-time monitoring of traffic behavior.

Data manipulation in manufacturing processes is another significant risk. An attacker who gains access to control systems could alter production parameters, modify sensor calibration, or even sabotage product quality without being immediately detected. Implementing secure communication protocols with end-to-end encryption protects the integrity of data transmitted between industrial devices. In addition, the use of digital logs and automated audits makes it possible to detect suspicious changes in production parameters and respond in time to possible manipulation attempts.

The human factor is one of the main vulnerabilities in manufacturing plant cybersecurity. Employees and operators can be targeted by social engineering attacks that seek to obtain access credentials or introduce malware into the network. Phishing campaigns targeting staff can facilitate the installation of malicious software on critical systems. Cybersecurity training and awareness of common threats can reduce the risk of employees being tricked by attackers. Implementing role-based access policies and restricting the use of removable devices such as USB drives help minimize the risks associated with human error.

Continuous monitoring is a fundamental strategy for protecting manufacturing plants from cyberattacks. Implementing intrusion detection systems allows for identifying anomalous network activity and generating real-time alerts in the event of possible attack attempts. Analysis of traffic behavior and correlation of events in different systems facilitates early detection of threats. Monitoring access logs and applying artificial intelligence to analyze unusual patterns improves incident response capabilities.

Industrial cybersecurity compliance is a key aspect to ensure the protection of manufacturing plants. Regulations such as IEC 62443 and NIST CSF establish guidelines on the implementation of security controls in industrial systems. Complying with these standards not only improves the security posture of the organization, but also facilitates collaboration with business partners and customers who require assurances on the security of production processes. Conducting security audits and periodically updating internal policies allows the infrastructure to be kept aligned with cybersecurity best practices.

Resilience of manufacturing plants to cyberattacks requires a combination of preventive measures, early detection and effective recovery plans. Redundancy in critical systems ensures continuity of production even in the event of an interruption caused by an attack. Developing incident response plans with clear procedures for containment, eradication and recovery of systems minimizes the impact of a cyberattack on the operation. Conducting simulations and response exercises allows for improved staff preparation and to evaluate the effectiveness of the protection strategies implemented.

Protecting manufacturing plants from cyberattacks is a challenge that requires a comprehensive and constantly evolving strategy. The increasing digitalization of industrial processes and the interconnectivity of devices increase exposure to cyber threats, making it essential to adopt security measures adapted to industrial environments. The combination of network segmentation, continuous monitoring, strong authentication and staff training makes it possible to reduce risks and ensure the security of operations in a world where cybersecurity is a key factor for the competitiveness and sustainability of modern manufacturing.

Security in Transportation Systems and Critical Infrastructure

Transport systems and critical infrastructure play an essential role in the economic and social stability of a country. Digitalisation and automation have enabled the optimisation of the operation of airports, railway networks, ports and urban transit systems, but have also introduced new vulnerabilities that can be exploited by malicious actors. Security in these environments requires a comprehensive approach that combines physical, cyber and operational measures to ensure service continuity and user protection.

The increasing interconnectivity of transport systems has increased the attack surface. Communication networks used to coordinate air traffic, manage trains and operate port infrastructure rely on digital systems that can be vulnerable to cyberattacks. An attacker who gains access to these systems could manipulate railway traffic signals, disrupt air navigation systems or disrupt logistics at a port. To mitigate these risks, it is essential to implement network segmentation, strict access control and secure communication protocols that prevent the manipulation of critical data.

Denial of service attacks pose a significant threat to transportation systems. This type of attack can affect the availability of traffic management platforms, ticketing systems, and communication platforms between operators and control centers. An attack targeting servers that manage information systems at airports or railway stations could lead to delays, disruptions, and chaos in operations. Implementing industrial firewalls, distributing services across redundant servers, and limiting external access are key strategies to mitigate the impact of these attacks.

Remote access to critical infrastructure is another vulnerable point in the security of transportation systems. Many operators and suppliers require remote access for monitoring and maintenance of equipment in subway stations, airport terminals, and railway control centers. Without adequate measures, these accesses can be exploited by attackers to infiltrate the network and manipulate key systems. Multi-factor authentication, the use of encrypted virtual private networks, and real-time monitoring of remote sessions are essential practices to reduce this risk.

Industrial control systems used in rail and air traffic management have been designed to operate with high availability and minimal latency, but in many cases they lack modern security mechanisms. Many of these systems were developed before cybersecurity was a central concern, so they use unencrypted communication protocols and do not feature robust authentication. Modernizing these systems and implementing solutions such as OPC UA with end-to-end encryption are necessary to improve infrastructure protection.

Malware targeting transportation infrastructure has increased in frequency and sophistication. A malware attack could disrupt communication between traffic control systems, manipulate sensors on runways, or disrupt logistics at cargo ports. Whitelisting applications, restricting unauthorized software from running, and continuously monitoring network activity can detect and block attacks before they cause significant damage.

Supply chain attacks are a growing concern in transportation infrastructure security. Many organizations rely on third-party vendors for hardware and software, which can introduce risks if these vendors' security controls are not properly assessed. An attacker who successfully compromises a traffic management system's software before it is installed could covertly gain access to critical infrastructure. Vendor validation, code inspection, and network segmentation that connects vendor systems to critical infrastructure help mitigate these types of threats.

Physical access to transport infrastructure must also be controlled with strict security measures. An attacker who gains access to a server room, railway control centre or air traffic control tower could directly manipulate the systems without the need for a cyber attack. Implementing biometric controls, video surveillance and role-based access segmentation minimises the risk of unauthorised access to critical areas.

The human factor is one of the biggest vulnerabilities in the security of transportation systems. Social engineering attacks, such as phishing, have been used to obtain access credentials to control systems and traffic management platforms. Training staff in cybersecurity, implementing awareness campaigns, and restricting access to critical information to authorized employees only are key measures to reduce this risk.

Real-time monitoring and threat detection improve the response capacity to incidents in critical infrastructures. The implementation of intrusion detection systems and behavioral analysis allows the identification of attack patterns before they affect operations. The correlation of events between control systems, traffic monitoring platforms and access logs facilitates the early detection of intrusion attempts and immediate response to incidents.

Regulatory compliance is a critical aspect of securing transportation systems and critical infrastructure. Regulations such as the NIS2 Directive in Europe and the NIST framework in the United States set guidelines for protecting critical infrastructure. Complying with these standards not only improves infrastructure security, but also facilitates collaboration with government agencies and other industry entities to share information on emerging threats.

Resilience of transportation systems to cyberattacks requires a combination of advanced technologies, segmentation strategies, and staff training. Redundancy in critical systems, the implementation of incident response plans, and the performance of cyberattack simulations can improve the ability to recover in the event of an intrusion. The adoption of artificial intelligence and machine learning in threat detection improves the ability to anticipate attacks and reduce their impact on infrastructure operations.

Protecting transportation systems and critical infrastructure is a challenge that requires a comprehensive and constantly evolving strategy. As the digitalization of these environments continues, it is essential to adopt security measures tailored to the specific risks of each sector. The combination of cybersecurity, physical security and regulatory compliance makes it possible to reduce vulnerabilities and ensure the stability and availability of essential services for society.

Vulnerability Management in Industrial Technology

Vulnerability management in industrial technology is an essential process for the protection of critical infrastructure and the operational continuity of control systems. Unlike information technology environments, where security updates and patching can be performed more frequently, in industrial systems these activities present additional challenges due to the need to ensure the stability and availability of processes. Identifying, assessing and mitigating vulnerabilities in these environments requires a structured approach that minimizes risks without compromising operations.

One of the main challenges in vulnerability management in industrial technology is the presence of legacy systems. Many critical infrastructures operate with equipment that has been in operation for decades and that was designed without considering cybersecurity. These systems use insecure communication protocols, lack robust authentication mechanisms, and in some cases cannot receive security updates due to compatibility restrictions. Network segmentation, the application of compensating controls, and the adoption of real-time monitoring solutions are fundamental strategies to mitigate the risks associated with these devices.

The first step in vulnerability management is identifying critical assets within the industrial environment. It is essential to have an up-to-date inventory of all devices connected to the network, including SCADA systems, programmable logic controllers, and industrial sensors. Lack of visibility into infrastructure assets increases the likelihood that vulnerable devices will remain unprotected. Implementing asset management and network scanning tools can detect outdated devices, assess insecure configurations, and prioritize corrective action based on risk level.

Vulnerability analysis in industrial technology must be carried out carefully to avoid operational disruptions. In IT environments, penetration tests and aggressive security scans can be executed without significantly affecting system availability. However, in OT, these scans can generate unintended impacts on control devices and production. To mitigate these risks, it is advisable to use passive monitoring approaches that allow vulnerabilities to be identified without interfering with system operation. Security assessments should be planned in coordination with operations teams to avoid impacts on infrastructure.

Vulnerability prioritization is a key aspect of risk management in industrial environments. Not all vulnerabilities represent the same level of threat, so it is necessary to assess the potential impact and probability of exploitation before implementing corrective measures. Factors such as the criticality of the affected system, the existence of known exploits, and the connectivity of the device within the network must be considered in the risk classification. The adoption of methodologies such as the CVSS (Common Vulnerability Scoring System) facilitates the objective evaluation of vulnerabilities and allows resources to be efficiently allocated to the most urgent mitigations.

Mitigating vulnerabilities in industrial technology cannot always be done through the application of security patches. In many cases, control systems operate with proprietary software or custom versions that cannot be updated without extensive validation. In addition, compatibility testing and certification of updates can be lengthy and costly processes in industrial environments. To address these limitations, it is essential to implement compensating controls such as network segmentation, access restriction, application whitelisting, and continuous monitoring of device activity.

Access control and credential management are essential measures to reduce exposure to exploitable vulnerabilities. Many vulnerabilities in OT environments are related to the use of default passwords, weak credentials, or overly permissive access configurations. Implementing multi-factor authentication, regular password rotation, and adopting the principle of least privilege minimizes the risk of unauthorized access. Additionally, removing inactive accounts and regularly auditing access can identify and correct insecure configurations before they are exploited by attackers.

Continuous monitoring and anomaly detection are key tools for early identification of vulnerability exploitation attempts. Implementing intrusion detection systems in industrial networks makes it possible to identify attack patterns and generate real-time alerts in the event of suspicious activity. The integration of artificial intelligence and machine learning in these solutions facilitates the identification of emerging threats and enables the application of automatic responses to contain incidents before they affect operations.

Collaboration with industrial technology vendors and manufacturers is a crucial aspect of vulnerability management. Many OT infrastructures rely on software and hardware developed by third parties, meaning that the responsibility for security does not lie solely with the operating organization. Maintaining constant communication with vendors and requiring vulnerability management processes within service agreements helps ensure that devices receive security updates and that risks are effectively mitigated.

Regulatory compliance and the adoption of cybersecurity standards reinforce vulnerability management in industrial environments. Standards such as IEC 62443, NIST 800-82, and the NIS2 Directive establish guidelines on the identification, assessment, and mitigation of vulnerabilities in control systems. Complying with these standards not only improves the organization's security posture, but also facilitates cooperation with regulatory entities and reduces exposure to sanctions or security incidents that may affect operational continuity.

Training staff in identifying and managing vulnerabilities is a fundamental component in protecting industrial infrastructures. Operators, engineers and system administrators must be trained in good security practices, detection of insecure configurations and incident response procedures. Conducting cyberattack simulations and security exercises improves the ability to react to threats and reinforces the cybersecurity culture within the organization.

Vulnerability management in industrial technology is an ongoing process that requires the implementation of strategies tailored to the specificities of OT systems. The combination of up-to-date inventories, risk analysis, compensating controls, real-time monitoring, and regulatory compliance can reduce the attack surface and ensure the resilience of critical infrastructures. As threats evolve, it is critical for organizations to take proactive approaches to identifying and mitigating vulnerabilities to protect the integrity and stability of their industrial operations.

Security in IoT and IIoT (Industrial Internet of Things) Devices

The Internet of Things and its industrial variant, the Industrial Internet of Things, have transformed the way technological infrastructures operate in multiple sectors. The incorporation of smart sensors, connected devices and real-time analysis platforms has made it possible to improve efficiency, optimize production and reduce operating costs. However, this interconnectivity has also introduced new cybersecurity risks that must be managed to avoid vulnerabilities that could compromise the operation of critical infrastructures.

One of the main challenges in IoT and IIoT device security is the lack of standardization in their design and communication. Many devices have been developed without incorporating adequate security measures, which makes them vulnerable to interception attacks, data manipulation and unauthorized access. The absence of robust authentication mechanisms and the use of insecure protocols in the transmission of information make it easier for attackers to compromise these devices and use them as entry points to infiltrate the network.

Access control to IoT and IIoT devices is a critical aspect of protecting them. Many of these devices still use default credentials or lack strong authentication, making them easy targets for automated attacks. Implementing multi-factor authentication and using digital certificates can reduce the risk of unauthorized access. Additionally, segmenting the network on which these devices operate minimizes the possibility that an attacker who compromises one of them can move laterally within the infrastructure and affect more critical systems.

Encrypting communications in IoT and IIoT devices is essential to ensure data integrity and confidentiality. Many devices use unencrypted protocols for information transmission, allowing attackers to intercept and manipulate critical data. Adopting secure protocols such as MQTT with TLS, OPC UA with end-to-end encryption, and digitally signing transmitted data are key strategies to strengthen communication security for these devices. Additionally, implementing role-based access controls ensures that only authorized systems can interact with connected devices.

Continuous monitoring and anomaly detection in IoT and IIoT devices makes it possible to identify suspicious activities before they can compromise infrastructure. Implementing specific intrusion detection systems for these devices makes it easier to identify anomalous traffic patterns and generate real-time alerts. AI-based behavioral analysis solutions can detect deviations in device operation and anticipate potential attacks before they cause disruptions to industrial processes.

Using application whitelists is an effective strategy to reduce the attack surface on IoT and IIoT devices. Unlike traditional malware detection systems, which rely on known threat signatures, whitelists only allow previously authorized software to run. This prevents malicious code from being installed on devices and reduces the chance of them being compromised by targeted attacks. Additionally, restricting access to unnecessary ports and removing unnecessary features on devices minimizes the risks of vulnerability exploitation.

Supply chain attacks have proven to be one of the biggest threats to the security of IoT and IIoT devices. Many manufacturers do not include security measures in their production processes, allowing attackers to compromise devices before they are delivered to the end user. Validating suppliers and implementing supply chain security audits are critical strategies to ensure that purchased devices do not contain backdoors or insecure configurations that can be exploited by attackers.

Ransomware has evolved to target IoT and IIoT devices, affecting the operation of factories, power plants, and transportation systems. A successful attack can block the functionality of sensors and control devices, causing disruptions to industrial processes. Implementing regular backups and setting up quick recovery mechanisms can minimize the impact of these attacks. Additionally, network segmentation and enforcing least-privilege access policies make it difficult for ransomware to spread within the infrastructure.

Regulatory compliance is a key aspect in securing IoT and IIoT devices. Regulations such as IEC 62443, NIST CSF, and the NIS2 Directive set specific requirements for the security of these devices in industrial environments. Meeting these standards not only improves infrastructure resilience, but also enables organizations to reduce exposure to emerging threats and improve confidence in deploying new technologies. Conducting security audits and implementing risk assessments can identify vulnerabilities and strengthen security controls before they can be exploited by attackers.

Maintaining and updating IoT and IIoT devices is a critical task in protecting them. Many devices do not receive security updates on a regular basis, leaving vulnerabilities exposed that can be exploited by attackers. Implementing a patch management process and scheduling firmware updates can reduce the risk of vulnerability exploitation. In cases where devices cannot be updated, adopting compensating controls such as network segmentation and access restriction minimizes the risks associated with lack of updates.

The human factor remains a key element in the security of IoT and IIoT devices. Lack of cybersecurity training can lead to incorrect configurations or the use of weak credentials that compromise the security of the devices. Continuous training of the personnel in charge of managing these devices and awareness of the most common threats can reduce the risk of successful attacks. In addition, the implementation of attack simulations and incident response exercises improves the organization's ability to react to possible security compromises.

Security in IoT and IIoT devices is a challenge that requires a combination of technical strategies, access controls, continuous monitoring and regulatory compliance. The growing adoption of these technologies in industrial and critical environments makes it essential to implement security measures that protect the infrastructure against cyberattacks. Network segmentation, communications encryption, anomaly detection and device updating are fundamental pillars to guarantee the integrity and availability of these systems in an interconnected world.

Cryptography and Encryption in Industrial Environments

Cryptography and encryption play a fundamental role in protecting information in industrial environments, where data integrity, confidentiality and authenticity are essential to ensure the security and stability of processes. The increasing digitalization of control systems, the interconnectivity of industrial devices and the integration with corporate networks have increased the need to adopt cryptographic mechanisms that protect communications and prevent unauthorized access. However, the implementation of cryptography in industrial environments presents unique challenges due to the latency, compatibility and performance constraints that characterize these systems.

One of the main objectives of encryption in industrial environments is to ensure the confidentiality of information transmitted between sensors, actuators, controllers and monitoring systems. In many industrial infrastructures, data is communicated without encryption using legacy protocols that were designed in an era when cybersecurity was not a priority. This allows attackers to intercept, modify and manipulate transmitted data through man-in-the-middle (MITM) attacks, which can compromise the operation of the infrastructure. Adopting secure protocols with end-to-end encryption is one of the most effective strategies to prevent these threats.

The use of robust encryption algorithms in communication between industrial devices helps protect the integrity and authenticity of data. Algorithms such as AES (Advanced Encryption Standard) with 256-bit keys have proven highly effective in protecting data in transit and at rest. In environments where speed and latency are critical factors, optimized variants of these algorithms can be used to ensure that security does not impact the performance of control systems. The combination of symmetric and asymmetric encryption allows data processing efficiency to be balanced with advanced information protection.

Authentication is another key aspect of using cryptography in industrial environments. Many operational technology devices still allow unauthenticated access or use default credentials, facilitating unauthorized access to critical systems. Implementing digital certificate-based authentication and using electronic signatures allows the identity of the devices involved in the communication to be verified, reducing the risk of identity theft and fraudulent access. Public key infrastructure (PKI) facilitates the issuance and management of digital certificates, ensuring that only authorized devices and users can access the industrial network.

Encryption at rest is an essential security measure to protect information stored on servers, databases, and industrial storage devices. In many critical infrastructures, operating logs, configuration parameters, and production data contain sensitive information that could be exploited by attackers if accessed without restrictions. Implementing encryption at rest using algorithms such as AES and using encryption keys protected by hardware security modules (HSMs) can ensure that data remains protected even in the event of physical theft or system compromise.

Using secure communication protocols with built-in encryption is an effective strategy to improve security in industrial environments. Protocols such as OPC UA (Open Platform Communications Unified Architecture) have been designed with advanced security capabilities, including end-to-end encryption, certificate-based authentication, and granular access control. Adopting these protocols in SCADA systems and programmable logic controllers ensures that information transmitted between industrial devices cannot be intercepted or altered by attackers.

One of the challenges in implementing cryptography in industrial environments is supporting legacy devices that do not support modern encryption mechanisms. In many infrastructures, upgrading or replacing these devices is not a viable option due to cost constraints or operational requirements. To address this issue, layered encryption solutions can be implemented, using security gateways that act as intermediaries between legacy devices and modern systems. These gateways can encrypt and authenticate communications without requiring modification of the original devices, improving the security of the infrastructure without affecting its operability.

Cryptographic key management is a critical aspect of industrial system security. Poor key management can lead to the exposure of encrypted data or the inability to recover information in the event of key loss. Implementing secure key management solutions, including the use of hardware security modules and periodic key rotation, can ensure the security of encrypted data. Additionally, network segmentation and restricting access to key management systems minimize the risk of these credentials being compromised.

Monitoring and anomaly detection in industrial cryptography implementations are critical to identifying potential attack attempts or misconfigurations. Integrating encrypted traffic analysis tools allows suspicious patterns to be detected without the need to decrypt transmitted information, ensuring that data remains protected while network activity is monitored. Correlating events in monitoring systems and periodically auditing cryptographic infrastructure helps maintain an optimal level of security and detect potential gaps before they can be exploited by attackers.

Compliance with cybersecurity regulations and standards reinforces the adoption of cryptography in industrial environments. Regulations such as IEC 62443, NIST 800-82, and the NIS2 Directive establish specific requirements for data protection through encryption and authentication in operational technology environments. Compliance with these regulations not only improves infrastructure security, but also facilitates collaboration with suppliers, business partners, and regulatory bodies in protecting critical infrastructure. Adopting best practices in cryptography and certifying industrial devices and systems helps ensure that deployed solutions meet the highest security standards.

Training staff in the proper use of cryptography and encryption is a determining factor for the success of its implementation in industrial environments. Operators, engineers and system administrators must be familiar with the basic principles of cryptography, the importance of key management and best practices in data protection. Continuous training and the performance of attack simulations allow for improved incident response and reinforce the cybersecurity culture within the organization.

The application of cryptography and encryption in industrial environments is a fundamental strategy to protect the integrity and confidentiality of information in highly interconnected environments. The adoption of robust algorithms, the implementation of secure protocols, adequate key management and continuous monitoring can reduce the risks associated with cyberattacks and ensure the security of critical infrastructures. As threats evolve, it is essential that organizations adapt their encryption strategies and strengthen their protection capabilities to face the challenges of the digital environment.

Supplier Assessment and Supply Chain Security

Supply chain security is a critical aspect in protecting industrial infrastructures and operational technology systems. As organizations increasingly rely on third parties for the provision of hardware, software and services, the risk of security compromises increases significantly. A single vulnerable point in the supply chain can become a gateway for attackers looking to infiltrate a company's infrastructure without needing to exploit internal vulnerabilities. Rigorous vendor evaluation and the implementation of security controls throughout the supply chain are essential to minimize the associated risks.

One of the main challenges in supply chain security is the lack of visibility into the security processes and measures adopted by suppliers. Many organizations rely on third parties without thoroughly assessing the strength of their cybersecurity controls, which can lead to significant security breaches. Attackers have identified this vulnerability and have used strategies such as manipulating software and hardware at the manufacturing stage to introduce malicious code into products before they reach the end customer. An example of this type of attack occurred with the SolarWinds malware, which managed to compromise multiple organizations through a legitimate software update that had been altered at source.

To mitigate these risks, it is essential to establish a vendor evaluation process based on security criteria. Before selecting a vendor, organizations should conduct security audits that include an analysis of their data protection policies, vulnerability management, and implementation of access controls on their systems. It is advisable to require vendors to have recognized certifications, such as ISO 27001 or IEC 62443, that validate their compliance with international security standards. In addition, signing service level agreements (SLAs) that include cybersecurity clauses ensures that vendors are committed to maintaining an adequate level of protection.

Continuous supplier monitoring is a key practice to detect potential supply chain security threats. It is not enough to assess suppliers at the time of contracting; periodic reviews are necessary to ensure that they continue to comply with established security requirements. Implementing risk assessment systems based on threat intelligence makes it possible to identify potential security gaps in the supply chain before they are exploited by attackers. In addition, collaborating with other industry players to share information on security incidents and emerging threats strengthens collective resilience against targeted attacks.

Supplier access to industrial infrastructure is another critical point in supply chain security. Many organizations allow third parties to remotely access control systems and production devices to perform maintenance or upgrades. Without adequate controls, these accesses can be used by attackers to infiltrate the network and compromise critical systems. Implementing multi-factor authentication, using secure connections via encrypted VPNs, and restricting access only to specific periods minimizes the risks associated with remote access management by suppliers.

Devices and hardware components purchased from third parties also pose a significant risk to supply chain security. The possibility of an attacker modifying devices during manufacturing to include backdoors or hidden vulnerabilities is a real threat that can compromise the security of an entire infrastructure. To reduce this risk, organizations should assess the provenance of purchased components and work only with trusted suppliers who follow strict quality and security controls in their production processes. Performing security audits on devices before they are integrated into the infrastructure can identify potential tampering before it can be exploited.

Managing vendor-provided security updates and patches is another key aspect of supply chain protection. Many organizations rely on third parties for the provision of software and firmware, meaning that any vulnerabilities in these products can directly impact their infrastructure. Establishing procedures to validate the authenticity of updates before deployment and preventing the installation of software from unverified sources is essential. Additionally, having a structured process for patching minimizes exposure to attacks that exploit known vulnerabilities in third-party products.

The human factor is one of the biggest vulnerabilities in supply chain security. Social engineering attacks targeting supplier employees can allow attackers to gain access to sensitive information or credentials for critical systems. Training staff in good cybersecurity practices and raising awareness of common threats, such as phishing and identity theft, are essential to reducing these risks. Requiring suppliers to implement cybersecurity training programs and adopt strict access control policies strengthens the security of the entire supply chain.

Regulatory compliance is a key factor in supply chain security management. Regulations such as the NIS2 Directive in Europe and the NIST framework in the United States establish specific requirements for supplier assessment and risk management in critical infrastructures. Ensuring compliance with these regulations not only improves the security of the organization, but also facilitates cooperation with government entities and other industry players to mitigate large-scale threats.

Supply chain resilience to cyberattacks requires a comprehensive approach that combines risk assessment, continuous monitoring, and strict access controls. Network segmentation and restricted privileges on critical systems limit the ability of a compromised supplier to impact infrastructure security. Adopting advanced technologies, such as artificial intelligence and behavioral analytics, can detect anomalies in supplier interactions and anticipate potential threats.

Supply chain security is a constantly evolving challenge that requires adapting strategies and collaboration across organizations to address emerging threats. Implementing rigorous supplier assessment processes, adopting security standards, and continuous risk monitoring strengthens the protection of industrial infrastructures and minimizes exposure to targeted cyberattacks. The combination of technology, security policies, and staff training makes it possible to ensure supply chain integrity and operational continuity in an increasingly interconnected environment.

Regulatory Compliance: IEC 62443, NIST and Other Standards

Compliance with cybersecurity regulations and standards in operational technology is a fundamental aspect to ensure the protection of critical infrastructures and industrial systems. Cyber threats targeting these environments have grown in frequency and sophistication, which has driven the creation of specific regulations to strengthen the security of control systems and industrial technology. Standards such as IEC 62443, the NIST cybersecurity framework, and the NIS2 Directive establish clear guidelines for the identification, mitigation, and response to threats in industrial environments. Adopting these standards not only improves infrastructure security, but also allows organizations to comply with regulatory requirements and improve their resilience to cyberattacks.

IEC 62443 is one of the most comprehensive frameworks for cybersecurity in operational technology. Developed by the International Electrotechnical Commission, this standard establishes an approach based on security levels and infrastructure segmentation to mitigate risks. Its structure is composed of different parts that cover everything from governance and risk management to the specific protection of industrial devices and networks. Implementing IEC 62443 allows for establishing security controls in SCADA systems, programmable logic controllers and automation networks, ensuring that each layer of the infrastructure has adequate defense mechanisms.

One of the key principles of IEC 62443 is the adoption of a defence-in-depth model, which involves applying multiple layers of security to reduce the likelihood of a full system compromise. This includes network segmentation, strong authentication, malware protection and continuous monitoring of network activity. The standard also introduces the concept of zones and conduits, which defines the separation of different systems within an infrastructure and the implementation of security barriers to control communication between them. This segmentation minimises the possibility of lateral movement in the network and makes it more difficult for an attack to spread should a system be compromised.

The NIST (National Institute of Standards and Technology) cybersecurity framework is another widely used standard in critical infrastructure protection. Its approach is based on five main functions: identification, protection, detection, response, and recovery. This methodology allows organizations to develop a comprehensive cybersecurity plan that addresses everything from risk assessment to incident management and infrastructure recovery after an attack. The flexibility of the NIST framework makes it applicable to different industrial sectors, facilitating its adoption by both private companies and government entities.

One of the most valuable elements of the NIST framework is its focus on risk management. Rather than prescribing specific controls, the framework provides a structure that allows organizations to assess their vulnerabilities and define security measures based on their risk profile. This allows for customized implementation that is adaptable to the reality of each infrastructure, ensuring that security controls are proportional to the threats the organization faces. In addition, the framework promotes the integration of advanced threat monitoring and detection technologies, enabling a proactive response to security incidents.

The NIS2 Directive, adopted by the European Union, is another key regulation in critical infrastructure cybersecurity. This regulation obliges operators of essential services and digital providers to implement rigorous security controls to protect their networks and systems. NIS2 expands the scope of its predecessor NIS by including more industrial sectors within its regulation and establishing more severe sanctions in case of non-compliance. Its focus on international cooperation and the exchange of threat information strengthens the resilience of the digital ecosystem across Europe.

Compliance with cybersecurity regulations involves not only the implementation of technical controls, but also the adoption of management and governance policies. Standards such as ISO 27001 establish specific requirements for information security management, including the identification of critical assets, vulnerability management and incident response. Its approach based on continuous improvement allows organizations to adjust their cybersecurity strategies progressively and in line with the evolution of threats.

Compliance with these standards also implies the need for regular security audits and assessments. Conducting penetration tests, attack simulations and compliance audits can identify security gaps before they are exploited by attackers. These assessments also help organizations demonstrate their commitment to cybersecurity to customers, regulators and business partners, strengthening trust in their industrial processes.

Implementing cybersecurity regulations and standards in industrial environments also requires staff training. System operators and administrators must be trained in security best practices, incident management, and the application of technical controls within their areas of responsibility. Conducting regular simulations and training can improve the organization's preparedness for cyberattacks and reduce the risk of human errors that could compromise the security of the infrastructure.

Integrating multiple standards into a single cybersecurity model enables organizations to strengthen their defenses more effectively. While IEC 62443 provides a specific approach to protecting industrial control systems, the NIST framework enables flexible and adaptable risk management. Combining these approaches with regulations such as NIS2 and ISO 27001 creates a robust security ecosystem that covers both technical protection and organizational management of cybersecurity risks.

Evolving cyber threats and the increasing interconnectivity of industrial systems make regulatory compliance a dynamic process. Organizations must stay up to date with new versions of standards and adapt their cybersecurity strategies based on changes in the threat landscape. Taking a proactive approach to regulatory implementation and investing in early detection and response technologies can improve the resilience of critical infrastructure and ensure operational continuity in an increasingly complex digital environment.

Security Monitoring and Supervision in OT Environments

Security monitoring and supervision in operational technology environments is critical to detecting threats, preventing incidents, and ensuring operational continuity of industrial and critical infrastructures. Unlike IT systems, where monitoring solutions are widely deployed, in OT monitoring must balance security with process stability. The availability of industrial systems is a priority, so any monitoring activity must be performed without affecting the performance of control devices or compromising production.

One of the biggest challenges in OT security monitoring is the diversity of devices and protocols used in these environments. Many industrial control systems operate with proprietary technologies that were not designed with advanced monitoring capabilities. In addition, some critical devices, such as programmable logic controllers, do not natively generate activity logs or use protocols that lack authentication and encryption mechanisms. To address these limitations, it is critical to implement monitoring solutions designed specifically for OT, capable of interpreting industrial traffic without generating interruptions in the operation.

Monitoring network traffic in OT environments allows for the identification of anomalous communication patterns that could indicate the presence of threats. Network segmentation is a key strategy to facilitate monitoring, allowing for the definition of security zones where differentiated controls can be applied based on the criticality of the systems. By implementing monitoring sensors at strategic points, it is possible to detect unauthorized access attempts, changes in device configuration, and anomalies in communication between control systems. The adoption of OT-specific intrusion detection technologies facilitates the identification of targeted attacks without generating false positives that affect operation.

The use of behavioral analytics is one of the most effective tools to improve threat detection in industrial environments. Instead of relying solely on known threat signatures, behavioral analytics makes it possible to establish a baseline of normal traffic and detect deviations that could indicate malicious activity. For example, an attempted communication between an IT system and a control device could be a sign of an ongoing attack, especially if that type of connection is not common within the infrastructure. Implementing artificial intelligence and machine learning in these solutions makes it possible to identify complex attack patterns that could go undetected with traditional monitoring techniques.

Event logging and auditing in industrial control systems are essential for security monitoring. Log collection allows the sequence of events to be reconstructed in the event of an incident and facilitates the identification of vulnerabilities exploited by attackers. However, in OT environments, log management presents challenges due to storage limitations and the need to ensure system performance. To mitigate these issues, it is recommended to implement centralized log management solutions, where logs from control devices, SCADA servers, and workstations are stored on a secure platform that is accessible to cybersecurity teams.

Real-time monitoring of access to critical systems is a key measure to prevent intrusions in industrial environments. Remote access to OT infrastructures has increased significantly with the digitalization of processes, which has increased the risks of targeted attacks. Implementing monitoring solutions that record and analyze each remote session makes it possible to detect suspicious access and prevent tampering with control devices. In addition, applying multi-factor authentication and restricting remote access only to previously authorized devices strengthens the protection of the infrastructure against unauthorized access.

Integrity monitoring in industrial devices is another fundamental strategy for OT security. Many attacks seek to modify the configuration of control systems to alter their operation without being detected. The implementation of integrity monitoring mechanisms makes it possible to detect changes in configuration files, firmware and software of industrial devices. Any unauthorized modification can generate automatic alerts and activate response protocols to avoid impacts on production.

OT-specific security operations centers have emerged as an effective solution for continuous monitoring of critical infrastructure. Unlike IT operations centers, which typically focus on protecting data and digital infrastructure, OT security centers are designed to detect threats that could compromise the stability of industrial systems. Integrating network monitoring, log analysis, intrusion detection, and incident response tools into a single environment makes security management easier and enables faster reaction to emerging threats.

Regulatory compliance is a key factor in OT security monitoring and supervision. Standards such as IEC 62443 and the NIST framework establish specific requirements for the monitoring of industrial systems, including the implementation of traffic monitoring, event auditing, and anomaly detection. Ensuring compliance with these standards not only improves the security of the infrastructure, but also facilitates cooperation with regulatory bodies and customers who require assurances on the protection of industrial processes.

Training staff in security monitoring is a critical element to ensure effective threat detection. Many incidents in industrial environments are not immediately identified due to a lack of awareness of OT attack indicators. Training operators and security teams in interpreting anomalous events, using monitoring tools, and responding to incidents improves the organization's ability to detect and mitigate threats in real time.

Using threat intelligence in OT environment monitoring helps improve the detection of specific attacks targeting industrial infrastructure. Gathering and analyzing information about recent attacks, threat actors, and vulnerabilities exploited in other sectors helps anticipate potential risks. Integrating threat intelligence with monitoring tools helps automate detection and response to tactics used in previous attacks, reducing reaction time and minimizing the impact of security incidents.

Security monitoring in OT environments requires a combination of advanced detection strategies, network segmentation, event auditing, and staff training. The digitalization of industrial systems has increased exposure to cyberattacks, so the implementation of monitoring solutions adapted to the characteristics of operational technology is essential for the protection of critical infrastructures. The adoption of behavioral analysis, threat intelligence, and integrity monitoring technologies strengthens the resilience of industrial environments against emerging threats, ensuring the stability and security of processes in an increasingly interconnected world.

Hardening and Protection of Industrial Equipment

Hardening and protecting industrial equipment is critical to ensuring the security and stability of control systems in critical infrastructure. Unlike in information technology environments, where devices can receive frequent security updates and be more easily replaced, in operational technology, equipment often operates for decades with configurations that are rarely changed. This longevity and operational stability can become vulnerabilities if adequate security hardening measures are not implemented to reduce the attack surface.

Hardening industrial equipment involves applying security settings that limit exposure to threats without affecting system availability. Many industrial infrastructures continue to operate with default configurations that were designed to facilitate interoperability and connectivity, but do not incorporate advanced protection measures. Removing unnecessary services, disabling unused ports, and implementing strict access controls are some of the first steps to strengthen the security of these devices.

One of the biggest risks in industrial equipment is the use of default credentials. Many devices, such as programmable logic controllers and SCADA servers, are deployed with passwords that have not been changed since installation. This makes it easy for attackers with access to preconfigured credential databases to infiltrate the network and compromise critical systems. Updating credentials, implementing multi-factor authentication, and centralized access management significantly reduce the risk of unauthorized access.

Network segmentation is an essential strategy in the hardening of industrial equipment. In many environments, industrial control systems share networks with IT or Internet-facing devices, which increases the possibility of attacks. Separating industrial networks using VLANs and implementing OT-specific firewalls limits traffic between devices and prevents lateral movement in case an attacker manages to infiltrate the infrastructure. In addition, applying the Zero Trust model reinforces security by verifying each connection before granting access to the systems.

Role-based access control is an effective protective measure to limit the exposure of industrial equipment to unauthorized users. In many plants, operators, engineers, and maintenance personnel require different levels of access to control systems. Assigning least privileges ensures that each user can only interact with the functions strictly necessary for their job. Removing inactive accounts and periodically auditing access help prevent old credentials from being used in targeted attacks.

Continuous monitoring of the status of industrial equipment is a key strategy for early detection of anomalies and potential attack attempts. Implementing behavioral analysis tools makes it possible to identify deviations in device operation, such as changes in configurations or unusual access attempts. Using activity logs and real-time monitoring makes it easier to detect security incidents before they can compromise production.

Software hardening in industrial equipment is another key aspect of hardening. Many devices run operating systems and applications that do not receive regular security updates. Patching and updating firmware can be complex processes in industrial environments, as any modifications must be validated to ensure they do not affect system stability. However, the lack of updates leaves open vulnerabilities that can be exploited by attackers. Planning secure update cycles and implementing application whitelists can reduce these risks without affecting operability.

Data and communications encryption is an essential protective measure in the security of industrial equipment. Many protocols used in OT do not include encryption by default, allowing attackers to intercept and manipulate critical information. Adopting secure protocols such as OPC UA with TLS encryption and implementing VPNs for remote connections reinforce the protection of data transmitted between devices. Additionally, using hardware security modules on critical devices allows cryptographic keys and credentials to be stored securely, reducing the risk of security compromises.

Isolating vulnerable industrial devices is an effective strategy to protect older systems that cannot be updated. In many infrastructures, equipment from decades ago is still in operation and cannot receive security patches. Implementing OT-specific firewalls, restricting network traffic, and monitoring access to these devices minimizes the risk of being exploited by attackers. Additionally, virtualizing certain systems allows devices to be emulated in controlled environments, reducing the exposure of obsolete hardware.

Integrating incident response mechanisms into the hardening of industrial equipment is essential to ensure rapid recovery from attacks. Implementing segmented backups and defining restoration procedures can mitigate the impact of security incidents. Running attack simulations and performing recovery tests help improve infrastructure resilience and reduce downtime in the event of a system compromise.

Regulatory compliance plays a key role in hardening and protecting industrial equipment. Standards such as IEC 62443 and NIST 800-82 establish specific requirements for the security of industrial control systems. Complying with these standards ensures that devices deployed in the infrastructure comply with adequate protection measures and that security management processes are aligned with industry best practices. Conducting compliance audits and updating security policies are essential elements to keep the infrastructure protected against emerging threats.

Training staff in best practices for hardening and OT security is a key element to the success of any protection strategy. Operators and system administrators must be familiar with secure device configuration, vulnerability identification, and incident response procedures. Conducting regular training and raising awareness of cyber risks can strengthen the security culture within the organization and reduce the likelihood of human errors that can compromise the infrastructure.

Hardening and protecting industrial equipment requires a combination of technical strategies, access controls, continuous monitoring and regulatory compliance. The digitalization of industrial systems has increased exposure to cyberattacks, so it is essential to implement security measures adapted to OT environments. Eliminating insecure configurations, restricting access, segmenting networks and constant monitoring can reduce the attack surface and ensure the stability of critical infrastructures against increasingly sophisticated threats.

Integration of SOCs with OT Environments

The integration of security operations centers with operational technology environments has become an essential aspect of protecting critical and industrial infrastructures. As cyber threats evolve and attacks targeting industrial control systems become more frequent, there is a need for centralized monitoring capable of detecting, analyzing, and responding to security incidents in real time. However, the convergence between information technology and operational technology environments presents specific challenges that must be addressed to achieve effective integration without affecting the stability of industrial processes.

One of the main challenges in integrating a SOC with OT is the difference in operational objectives of both environments. In IT, data confidentiality and integrity are key priorities, while in OT, system availability is the most critical factor. Applying traditional IT security measures in OT can lead to operational disruptions, affecting production and the efficiency of industrial processes. For this reason, it is essential to adapt monitoring and incident response strategies to the particularities of industrial control systems, avoiding any action that may compromise operational continuity.

Security monitoring in OT environments requires efficient data collection that can identify suspicious events without overloading the infrastructure. Many industrial devices, such as programmable logic controllers and SCADA systems, have limited capabilities to record security events, making early detection of attacks difficult. To address this issue, it is necessary to deploy passive monitoring sensors that can analyze network traffic without interfering with the operation of the devices. Correlating events between these sensors and threat detection systems enables more effective monitoring and reduces the possibility of false positives.

Network segmentation is a key strategy to facilitate the integration of SOCs with OT environments. Separating industrial networks from corporate networks using security zones and specialized firewalls allows for establishing control points where traffic can be inspected without compromising system stability. Additionally, implementing demilitarized networks between the SOC and industrial control systems helps minimize the exposure of OT devices to external threats and limits the ability of attackers to move laterally within the infrastructure.

Behavioral analytics is a fundamental tool in the integration of SOCs with industrial environments. Rather than relying solely on known threat signatures, behavioral analytics makes it possible to detect deviations in normal system activity, identifying anomalous patterns that could indicate an attack in progress. For example, an attempt to access an industrial controller from an unauthorized IP address or an unexpected change in a sensor configuration can be signs of a possible intrusion. Integrating artificial intelligence into the SOC makes it possible to improve threat detection and automate incident responses in real time.

Remote access to industrial systems is one of the most critical attack vectors in OT cybersecurity. SOC integration with industrial environments must include rigorous monitoring of remote connections to detect suspicious access and prevent the use of compromised credentials. Implementing multi-factor authentication and restricting access to only authorized devices reinforces infrastructure security. Additionally, real-time analysis of remote sessions makes it possible to detect anomalous behavior and trigger automatic responses to mitigate potential threats before they become major incidents.

Incident management in OT environments requires response protocols tailored to the criticality of industrial systems. Unlike IT environments, where security incidents can be resolved by disconnecting affected devices or immediately applying patches, in OT any interruption in operation can have serious consequences for production. The integration of a SOC with OT must include tiered response procedures that allow threats to be contained without affecting operational continuity. Implementing application whitelists and isolating compromised devices through dynamic network segmentation are effective strategies to minimize the impact of incidents.

Regulatory compliance is a key factor in the integration of SOCs with OT environments. Regulations such as IEC 62443, NIST 800-82, and the NIS2 Directive establish specific requirements for security monitoring in industrial systems. Ensuring that the SOC complies with these regulations not only improves the security of the infrastructure, but also facilitates cooperation with regulatory bodies and customers who require assurances on the protection of industrial processes. Automated security reporting and continuous event auditing allow for demonstrating compliance with standards and improving the security posture of the organization.

Staff training is a fundamental element to ensure effective integration between SOCs and OT environments. Operators and security teams must be trained in identifying threats in industrial systems, using monitoring tools, and applying incident response procedures. Conducting attack simulations and cybersecurity exercises improves the organization's preparedness for emerging threats and reduces the risk of human errors that could compromise the infrastructure.

Integrating SOCs with OT environments requires a combination of advanced monitoring strategies, network segmentation, behavioral analysis, and incident management tailored to the criticality of industrial systems. The growing interconnectivity of industrial processes has increased exposure to cyberattacks, making it essential to have centralized monitoring capable of detecting and mitigating threats in real time. The adoption of artificial intelligence technologies, the implementation of rigorous access controls, and staff training can strengthen the security of industrial infrastructures and ensure the resilience of systems against increasingly sophisticated cyberattacks.

Disaster Recovery Planning in Operational Technology

Disaster recovery planning in operational technology is an essential component of ensuring business continuity in industrial and critical infrastructure. Unlike in information technology environments, where data recovery and service resumption are often focused on digital aspects, in OT disruptions can directly impact production, worker safety, and infrastructure stability. A failure in industrial control systems can result in the shutdown of a manufacturing plant, disruption of power supply, or even the creation of hazardous conditions in critical facilities.

One of the main challenges in disaster recovery planning in OT is the coexistence of legacy equipment with new technologies. Many industrial systems were designed without considering cybersecurity or resilience to failures, which makes it difficult to implement modern recovery strategies. In addition, the diversity of devices, communication protocols and dependencies between systems means that restoration of operation must be carefully planned to avoid collateral damage or chain failures.

Identifying critical assets is the first step in disaster recovery planning in industrial environments. Not all systems have the same level of importance within the operation, so it is essential to establish priorities based on the impact that their interruption would have. SCADA systems, programmable logic controllers and security monitoring devices are usually considered high-priority assets, since their operation is essential for the stability of the infrastructure. Creating a detailed inventory of these assets allows appropriate recovery strategies to be defined for each one.

Risk assessment is another key element in OT recovery planning. Not all disasters have the same origin or impact, so it is necessary to identify the main risks that could compromise the operation. Threats can include targeted cyberattacks, failures in communication systems, human error, natural disasters or mechanical failures in critical equipment. Each of these scenarios requires a different recovery approach, so the risk assessment must consider both the operational impacts and the possible restoration times of the affected systems.

Recovery plans should include redundancy strategies that help minimize the impact of an interruption in operations. Implementing backup systems and duplicating critical infrastructure facilitates rapid recovery in the event of a failure. In OT, redundancy applies not only to servers and databases, but also to physical devices that control industrial processes. Having backup controllers, redundant sensors, and alternative power supplies can ensure business continuity even in crisis situations.

Backups are a fundamental component of any disaster recovery plan. However, in OT environments, backup management must be done in a way that does not affect the stability of control systems. The frequency of backups must be defined based on the criticality of the system and the frequency with which its configurations change. In addition, backups must be stored in secure environments and outside the production network to prevent them from being compromised in the event of a cyberattack. Periodic validation of these backups is essential to ensure their integrity and functionality in case they are needed for restoration.

Recovery time is a critical factor in OT disaster planning. Unlike IT systems, where services can be restored in a matter of hours, in OT a prolonged interruption can result in multimillion-dollar losses and affect the physical security of facilities. Specific recovery times must be established for each critical system and detailed procedures must be defined to restore operations in the shortest possible time. Conducting periodic recovery tests helps to evaluate the effectiveness of these procedures and identify opportunities for improvement.

Coordination between IT and OT teams is essential for effective disaster recovery. In many organizations, cybersecurity teams and industrial operations managers work independently, which can lead to conflicts when implementing recovery strategies. Integrating both teams into recovery planning helps ensure that restoration measures do not compromise the stability of industrial processes or the security of the infrastructure. Creating clear communication protocols and defining responsibilities within the recovery plan are key to avoiding delays and errors during incident response.

Recovery automation is an effective strategy to minimize the impact of OT outages. Implementing automatic response systems allows restoration mechanisms to be triggered without the need for human intervention, reducing downtime and ensuring more efficient recovery. Real-time monitoring systems can detect anomalies and trigger predefined recovery procedures, such as switching to backup systems or activating emergency protocols in the event of control system failures.

Regulatory compliance is a critical factor in disaster recovery planning in OT. Regulations such as IEC 62443, NIST 800-82, and the NIS2 Directive set specific requirements for managing resilience in industrial infrastructure. Complying with these standards not only improves an organization's resilience, but also facilitates cooperation with regulatory bodies and customers who require assurances on the protection of industrial processes. Detailed documentation of recovery plans and regular audits can demonstrate compliance with these regulations and improve incident preparedness.

Training staff in the execution of recovery plans is a key aspect to ensure their effectiveness. In an OT environment, the speed and accuracy of the response to an incident can make the difference between a controlled interruption and a large-scale crisis. Performing recovery simulations and exercises allows the reaction capacity of work teams to be evaluated and the procedures defined in the recovery plan to be optimized. Constantly updating these plans based on new threats and changes in the infrastructure is essential to maintain their effectiveness over time.

Disaster recovery planning for operational technology should be a continuous process that involves identifying risks, implementing redundancy strategies, coordinating between teams, and training staff. The resilience of industrial infrastructures depends on the ability of organizations to respond quickly and effectively to incidents that may compromise their stability. The adoption of advanced technologies, compliance with regulations, and the integration of well-defined recovery procedures can reduce the impact of disasters and ensure operational continuity in increasingly digitalized industrial environments exposed to emerging threats.

Simulation and Penetration Testing in OT Environments

Simulation and penetration testing in operational technology environments are critical tools for assessing the security of industrial infrastructures and detecting vulnerabilities before they can be exploited by attackers. As threats targeting industrial control systems increase in sophistication, organizations must adopt proactive assessment strategies to strengthen the protection of their critical assets. However, performing penetration testing in OT presents unique challenges due to the need to ensure the stability of operational processes and minimize the risk of production disruptions.

One of the main challenges in performing penetration testing in OT is the nature of industrial systems. Unlike in IT environments, where systems can be rebooted and patched with relative ease, in OT any disruption can affect the physical security of the infrastructure and result in significant financial losses. Many industrial devices operate on legacy software that cannot be updated without extensive compatibility testing. In addition, some SCADA systems and programmable logic controllers were not designed to withstand cyberattacks, increasing the risk of failure if testing is not done carefully.

To mitigate these risks, it is essential to adopt a structured approach to the execution of simulations and penetration tests in OT. Before carrying out any security assessment, it is necessary to define the scope of the analysis, identifying the assets to be assessed and the limits of the tests to avoid negative impacts on the operation. Segmenting environments allows testing to be carried out on simulated infrastructures or test networks before applying them to production systems, thus reducing the risk of affecting the stability of industrial processes.

Penetration testing in OT environments can be divided into several phases. The first stage involves gathering information about the infrastructure, including connected devices, protocols used, and security configurations implemented. This phase allows testers to identify potential weak points and define realistic attack strategies that can be used by malicious actors. Passive scanning is a key technique in this stage, as it allows obtaining data about the network without generating suspicious traffic that can affect the operation of industrial systems.

The second phase of penetration testing involves vulnerability assessment. At this stage, specialized tools are used to identify weaknesses in devices, applications, and network configurations. However, unlike in IT environments, where automated testing can be performed with relative ease, in OT a more controlled approach is recommended to avoid operational impacts. Testing should be performed in a laboratory environment whenever possible, and in case of production assessments, methodologies designed to minimize risk should be applied, such as manual configuration analysis and access policy assessment.

Controlled exploitation of vulnerabilities is a critical phase of OT penetration testing. Unlike attacks in IT environments, where systems can be quickly restored, any attempt at exploitation in OT must be carried out with extreme caution. Simulating attacks without affecting operations allows the effectiveness of security measures to be assessed without putting service continuity at risk. In many cases, it is recommended to use virtualized environments or replica systems to execute controlled attacks and assess incident response capabilities.

Anomaly detection is another key component in OT attack simulation. In many industrial environments, attacks do not result in immediate disruptions, but instead seek to alter operating parameters or subtly modify configurations to evade detection. Analyzing network traffic, comparing historical logs, and identifying device changes can detect malicious activity before it causes significant damage. Implementing security monitoring tools tailored to industrial protocols improves detection capabilities and enables a rapid response to intrusion attempts.

Attack simulation also plays a key role in training OT staff and validating incident response procedures. Conducting cybersecurity exercises helps assess the readiness of operational and security teams for real-life attack scenarios. Simulating ransomware attacks on industrial systems, testing responses to unauthorized remote access attempts, and executing denial-of-service attacks in controlled environments are practices that strengthen organizational resilience and improve coordination between IT and OT teams.

Regulatory compliance is another key factor in planning and executing penetration testing in OT environments. Standards such as IEC 62443 and the NIST Cybersecurity Framework provide guidelines on conducting security assessments on industrial infrastructures. Complying with these standards not only helps improve the security of the organization, but also facilitates cooperation with regulators and business partners who require assurances on the protection of industrial processes. Documenting test results and implementing remediation plans based on these assessments allows for continuous improvement of the organization's security posture.

Planning penetration tests in OT must consider the impact on the operation and the criticality of the tested systems. Running tests during off-peak hours, coordinating with operational teams, and implementing containment measures to avoid disruptions are key strategies to minimize risk. Conducting security audits and integrating penetration tests into risk management processes allows vulnerabilities to be detected and corrected before they can be exploited by attackers.

The evolution of cyber threats in industrial environments requires organizations to take a proactive approach to security assessment. Combining attack simulations, controlled penetration testing, and continuous network activity monitoring allows threats to be detected and mitigated before they impact operations. Integrating threat intelligence into security assessment processes improves the ability to anticipate new attack vectors and strengthens the protection of critical infrastructures in an increasingly digitalized world exposed to sophisticated cyber risks.

Cybersecurity in the Petrochemical and Gas Industry

The petrochemical and gas industry is a strategic sector with an infrastructure highly dependent on operational technology and industrial control systems. The digitalization of processes, the automation of refineries and remote monitoring of operations have improved efficiency and production, but have also increased exposure to cyber threats. Attacks on this sector can not only cause economic losses and disruptions to energy supply, but can also put the physical safety of workers and facilities at risk due to the manipulation of critical processes.

One of the main cybersecurity challenges in the petrochemical and gas industry is the convergence between IT and OT systems. Information technology networks, which manage administrative and business data, are increasingly connected to industrial control systems, expanding the attack surface. Attackers can exploit vulnerabilities in IT infrastructure to access operating systems, manipulate drilling equipment, alter pressure parameters or disrupt the flow of oil and gas. Network segmentation is a key strategy to minimize these risks, ensuring that critical systems are isolated from less secure networks.

Ransomware attacks represent one of the biggest threats to the industry. Cybercriminal groups have targeted refineries and pipelines, blocking critical systems and demanding payment for their restoration. In 2021, a ransomware attack on the Colonial Pipeline in the United States disrupted fuel supplies in several regions, demonstrating the industry's vulnerability to such threats. To mitigate these risks, organizations should implement backups on isolated systems, apply access segmentation, and restrict the use of administrative credentials to what is strictly necessary.

Remote access to oil and gas infrastructure is a significant attack vector. Engineers and suppliers need to connect to SCADA systems and monitoring devices from remote locations to perform maintenance and operational adjustments. Without proper controls, these accesses can be exploited by attackers to infiltrate the industrial network. Implementing multi-factor authentication, restricting remote access to authorized equipment only, and continuously monitoring remote sessions reduces the likelihood that a compromised account will be used to access critical systems.

Securing field devices in the petrochemical and gas industry is another major challenge. Sensors, actuators and programmable logic controllers are deployed in harsh environments, exposed to extreme conditions and, in many cases, without built-in security measures. The lack of encryption in communications between these devices and centralized control systems allows attackers to intercept or modify critical signals. Adopting secure protocols such as OPC UA with TLS encryption and device authentication using digital certificates strengthens the protection of these infrastructures.

Denial of service attacks can also severely impact the petrochemical and gas industry. These attacks seek to saturate the network with malicious traffic to disrupt communication between control systems and industrial devices. A disruption in the connectivity of a SCADA system can prevent real-time monitoring and adjustment of processes, increasing the risk of operational failures. Implementing industrial firewalls, traffic filtering, and monitoring for anomalous patterns in the network help detect and mitigate these types of threats before they impact the operation.

The human factor remains one of the main cybersecurity vulnerabilities in the petrochemical and gas industry. Social engineering attacks, such as phishing, have been used to obtain access credentials to critical systems. A single mistake by an employee clicking on a malicious link can compromise the security of the entire infrastructure. Cybersecurity training for operational and administrative staff is essential to reduce these risks. Conducting attack simulations and awareness exercises reinforces the teams' preparedness against attempts at psychological manipulation by attackers.

Continuous monitoring and threat monitoring can improve incident detection in oil and gas infrastructure. Implementing industrial-specific intrusion detection systems can identify attack patterns before they can impact operations. Integrating artificial intelligence into network monitoring makes it easier to detect anomalies in traffic and device behavior, enabling real-time responses to potential threats.

Regulatory compliance is a key aspect of cybersecurity in the petrochemical and gas sector. Regulations such as IEC 62443 and the NIST 800-82 framework establish specific requirements for the protection of critical infrastructure. Complying with these standards not only improves the security of operations, but also facilitates cooperation with regulatory bodies and customers who require assurances on the protection of infrastructure. Implementing security audits and documenting incidents can improve the organization's resilience and strengthen its ability to respond to emerging threats.

Forensic analysis of security incidents is a key tool for understanding the nature of an attack and preventing future intrusions. In the petrochemical and gas industry, where disruptions can result in multi-million dollar losses, it is essential to have investigation procedures that allow identifying the methods used by attackers. Collecting activity logs, analyzing network traffic, and reviewing device configurations help determine the origin of an incident and implement corrective measures.

The adoption of threat intelligence in cybersecurity in the petrochemical and gas sector allows anticipating targeted attacks. Malicious actors operating against this sector often use advanced tactics and customized attacks to compromise critical systems. The integration of global threat databases with monitoring systems allows detecting attack attempts based on patterns previously identified in other infrastructures. Collaboration with government agencies and industry associations strengthens the ability to defend against advanced cyber threats.

Cybersecurity in the petrochemical and gas industry requires a combination of advanced protection strategies, network segmentation, continuous monitoring and regulatory compliance. The increasing digitalization of processes and the interconnectivity of systems have increased exposure to cyberattacks, making it necessary to implement security measures adapted to industrial environments. Network segmentation, robust authentication, staff training and real-time monitoring can reduce risks and ensure the operational stability of this critical sector for the economy and global energy security.

Safety in Water and Sanitation Infrastructure

Water and sanitation infrastructure is a critical sector whose security is essential to ensure access to essential resources for the population and industry. The digitalization and automation of water supply and treatment systems have improved operational efficiency, but have also increased exposure to cyberattacks. Protecting these systems is vital, as an interruption in supply or tampering with sanitation processes can have serious consequences for public health and the environment.

One of the biggest challenges in water and wastewater infrastructure security is the reliance on SCADA systems and industrial control devices that were designed in an era when cybersecurity was not a priority. Many of these systems use unencrypted protocols and lack robust authentication, making them attractive targets for attackers looking to disrupt water supply or alter treatment quality. Modernizing these systems and adopting appropriate protective measures is essential to reduce the risks associated with their operation.

Targeted attacks on water systems have increased in recent years, demonstrating the vulnerability of these environments. On several occasions, malicious actors have attempted to modify control parameters, such as the dosing of chemicals in treatment plants, with the aim of contaminating the water supply. To mitigate these risks, it is essential to implement multi-factor authentication for access to critical systems, restrict user privileges, and monitor in real time any attempt at unauthorized manipulation of control systems.

Network segmentation is a key strategy in protecting water and wastewater infrastructure. In many cases, control systems operate on networks that are connected to administrative systems or exposed to the internet without adequate security measures. This lack of segmentation allows an attacker who compromises a corporate network to move laterally and access critical devices. Implementing industrial firewalls and separating networks using VLANs or demilitarized networks minimizes the attack surface and protects control systems from unauthorized access.

Ransomware has begun to pose a significant threat to the water and sanitation sector. Such an attack can block monitoring and control systems, preventing the monitoring of water flow, waste treatment and distribution to consumers. Implementing segmented backups, restricting administrative access and monitoring network traffic can mitigate the impact of such attacks and ensure rapid recovery of compromised systems.

Remote access to water infrastructure is another critical point in the sector's cybersecurity. Many treatment plants and pumping stations rely on remote access for monitoring and maintenance of their systems. However, poorly protected remote connections can become a gateway for attackers. Implementing VPN tunnels with strong encryption, multi-factor authentication, and real-time monitoring of remote sessions reduces the risk of unauthorized access and protects the integrity of operational systems.

Detecting anomalies in water and sanitation infrastructure is a key tool for preventing security incidents. Implementing AI-based monitoring systems makes it possible to identify unusual patterns in network traffic, access logs, and the operation of critical devices. A sudden variation in chlorine levels in water treatment or unexpected changes in distribution valves can be signs of an attempted attack. Correlating events at different levels of the infrastructure facilitates early detection of threats and enables a rapid response to avoid impacts on the operation.

Regulatory compliance is a key factor in the security of water and wastewater infrastructure. Regulations such as IEC 62443 and the NIST Cybersecurity Framework establish guidelines on the protection of critical industrial systems, including access management, network segmentation, and threat monitoring. Complying with these standards helps ensure infrastructure security, reduce exposure to attacks, and improve incident response capabilities. Conducting security audits and implementing controlled penetration tests helps identify vulnerabilities and strengthen system protection.

The human factor remains one of the biggest vulnerabilities in water and sanitation system security. Social engineering attacks, such as phishing, can be used to obtain access credentials to control systems or trick employees into executing malicious commands. Training staff in cybersecurity and raising awareness of common threats can reduce the likelihood of a successful attack. Implementing cyberattack simulations and conducting incident response exercises improves the preparedness of operational teams and strengthens the organization's resilience to targeted attacks.

Forensic analysis of water infrastructure security incidents helps determine the nature of an attack and prevent future intrusions. Collecting activity logs, analyzing network traffic, and reviewing configurations on control devices facilitates the identification of vulnerabilities exploited by attackers. Documenting these findings and applying corrective measures strengthens infrastructure security and improves the ability to respond to new attack attempts.

Integrating threat intelligence into water and sanitation infrastructure security enables anticipation of targeted attacks. Gathering and analyzing information on emerging threats, malicious actors, and vulnerabilities exploited in other sectors facilitates the implementation of more effective defense strategies. Collaboration with government agencies and industry associations enables sharing information on security incidents and strengthening the resilience of critical infrastructure.

Security in water and sanitation infrastructure requires a combination of technical measures, continuous monitoring, staff training and regulatory compliance. The increasing interconnectivity of these systems has increased exposure to cyberattacks, so it is essential to implement protection strategies adapted to industrial environments. Network segmentation, anomaly detection, access restriction and real-time monitoring can minimize risks and ensure the stability and reliability of water supply and treatment systems.

Security in Automation Networks and PLCs

Security in automation networks and programmable logic controllers is a critical aspect in protecting industrial infrastructures and automated processes. Automation has enabled efficiency improvements, cost reductions and production optimization in multiple sectors, but it has also introduced new vulnerabilities that can be exploited by attackers. PLCs play a fundamental role in industry, controlling essential equipment in manufacturing, energy, transportation and other critical sectors. An attack on these devices can compromise the safety of the operation, generate production failures and affect the integrity of the systems.

One of the main challenges in automation network security is the lack of protection mechanisms in legacy devices. Many PLCs were designed without considering cybersecurity as a priority, which has left numerous industrial infrastructures exposed. Some controllers still operate with default credentials, lack robust authentication, and use unencrypted communication protocols. This allows attackers to intercept and manipulate commands sent to these devices, altering the operation of control systems. Updating firmware, changing default passwords, and implementing multi-factor authentication are basic measures to reduce these risks.

Network segmentation is an essential strategy for protecting PLCs and automation networks. In many industrial environments, control systems are connected to corporate networks or exposed to the Internet without adequate security measures. This allows an attacker who compromises an administrative network to move laterally to control devices. Segmentation using VLANs, demilitarized networks, and industrial firewalls allows critical systems to be isolated and communication restricted to authorized devices and applications only. Applying the Zero Trust model to industrial networks strengthens security by verifying each access before allowing connection to control systems.

Automation network monitoring is a key tool for real-time threat detection. Traffic monitoring can identify unauthorized access attempts, changes to PLC configurations, and attack patterns targeting control systems. Implementing intrusion detection systems adapted to industrial environments facilitates the identification of suspicious activities and rapid response to security incidents. In addition, behavioral analysis based on artificial intelligence can detect anomalies in device operation and prevent tampering before they affect production.

Ransomware attacks pose a growing threat to automation networks and PLCs. Cybercriminals have begun developing ransomware variants specifically designed for industrial control systems, blocking access to PLCs and demanding payments to restore their operation. A successful attack can disrupt production lines, cause failures in automated processes, and cause significant financial losses. Network segmentation, implementing backups on isolated systems, and restricting administrative access are key strategies to mitigate these risks and ensure rapid recovery of affected devices.

Remote access to PLCs and automation networks is another critical point in industrial cybersecurity. Many companies allow engineers and technicians to access these devices from remote locations to perform maintenance and operational adjustments. Without proper controls, these connections can be used by attackers to infiltrate industrial infrastructure. Implementing encrypted VPN tunnels, multi-factor authentication, and real-time monitoring of remote sessions reduces the likelihood of unauthorized access and strengthens infrastructure security.

Using secure protocols in automation networks is critical to ensuring the integrity and confidentiality of communications between devices. Many PLCs and SCADA systems still use unencrypted protocols, allowing attackers to intercept and modify transmitted data. Adopting OPC UA with TLS encryption, implementing application whitelists, and digital certificate-based authentication protects communication between industrial devices and reduces exposure to threats.

The human factor remains one of the main vulnerabilities in automation network security. Social engineering attacks, such as phishing, can be used to obtain access credentials to PLCs or trick operators into executing malicious commands. Cybersecurity training for personnel who operate and maintain these systems is essential to reduce these risks. Conducting attack simulations and incident response exercises reinforces the readiness of operational teams and improves the ability to detect and respond to intrusion attempts.

Regulatory compliance is a key aspect of PLC and automation network security. Standards such as IEC 62443 and the NIST Cybersecurity Framework set specific requirements for protecting industrial control systems, including access management, network segmentation, and threat monitoring. Complying with these standards helps ensure infrastructure security, reduce exposure to attacks, and improve incident response capabilities. Conducting security audits and implementing controlled penetration tests helps identify vulnerabilities and strengthen the protection of control systems.

Forensic analysis of security incidents in automation networks helps determine the nature of an attack and prevent future intrusions. Collecting activity logs, analyzing network traffic, and reviewing configurations on control devices facilitates the identification of vulnerabilities exploited by attackers. Documenting these findings and applying corrective measures strengthens the security of the infrastructure and improves the ability to respond to new attack attempts.

Adopting threat intelligence in automation and PLC network security enables anticipation of targeted attacks. Gathering and analyzing information on emerging threats, malicious actors, and vulnerabilities exploited in other sectors facilitates the implementation of more effective defense strategies. Collaboration with government agencies and industry associations enables sharing information on security incidents and strengthening the resilience of critical infrastructure.

Security in automation networks and PLCs requires a combination of technical measures, continuous monitoring, staff training and regulatory compliance. The increasing interconnectivity of these systems has increased exposure to cyberattacks, so it is essential to implement protection strategies adapted to industrial environments. Network segmentation, anomaly detection, access restriction and real-time monitoring can minimize risks and ensure the stability and reliability of industrial automation systems.

Identification and Protection of Critical Assets

Identifying and protecting critical operational technology assets is an essential component of industrial cybersecurity. Critical assets include all those systems, devices, networks and processes whose interruption or alteration can significantly affect the operation, security and continuity of the business. In industrial and critical infrastructure environments, protecting these assets is a challenge due to the large number of connected devices, the coexistence of legacy technologies and the increasing interconnectivity with information technology networks.

The first step in identifying critical assets is to conduct a detailed inventory of all systems and devices that are part of the industrial infrastructure. Many organizations are unaware of all the equipment operating on their networks, which makes it difficult to implement effective security measures. Lack of visibility into assets exposes the infrastructure to unnecessary risk, as an attacker could exploit vulnerabilities in unprotected systems. Implementing asset management tools allows you to map the network, identify connected devices, and classify systems according to their level of criticality.

Once the assets have been identified, their impact on operations and security must be assessed. Not all devices have the same importance within the infrastructure, so a categorization process must be established based on criteria such as availability, integrity and confidentiality of the information they manage. SCADA systems, programmable logic controllers, monitoring sensors and physical security devices are usually considered high-priority assets, since their alteration could generate operational failures or affect the security of the facilities.

Network segmentation is one of the most effective strategies for protecting critical assets. In many industrial environments, control systems operate on networks shared with back-office devices or even those with Internet access, increasing the attack surface. Separating networks using VLANs, demilitarized networks, and industrial firewalls can isolate critical assets from less secure networks and reduce the possibility of unauthorized access. Implementing strict access controls ensures that only authorized systems and users can interact with these devices.

Authentication and access management play a critical role in protecting critical assets. In many industrial environments, devices still use default credentials or weak passwords, making it easier for attackers to gain access to sensitive systems. Adopting multi-factor authentication, centralized credential management, and assigning least privileges significantly reduces the risk of unauthorized access. Additionally, removing inactive accounts and regularly auditing access help detect and correct insecure configurations before they can be exploited.

Continuous monitoring of critical assets enables real-time threat detection and improved incident response capabilities. Implementing industrial-specific intrusion detection systems makes it easier to identify unauthorized access attempts, configuration changes, and suspicious traffic patterns. Real-time monitoring of device behavior enables anomalies to be identified before they can compromise operations. Using artificial intelligence in industrial network monitoring improves advanced threat detection capabilities and reduces incident response times.

Data and communications encryption is an essential measure for the protection of critical assets. Many industrial systems still use unencrypted protocols, allowing attackers to intercept and manipulate critical information. Adopting secure protocols such as OPC UA with TLS encryption and implementing digital signatures ensure the integrity and confidentiality of transmitted data. Furthermore, using hardware security modules on critical devices allows cryptographic keys and credentials to be stored securely, reducing the risk of security compromises.

Forensic analysis of security incidents is a key tool for protecting critical assets. Collecting activity logs, analyzing network traffic, and reviewing configurations on control devices can help determine the nature of an attack and prevent future intrusions. Documenting these findings and applying corrective measures strengthens infrastructure security and improves the ability to respond to new attack attempts.

Regulatory compliance is a key factor in identifying and protecting critical assets. Regulations such as IEC 62443, NIST 800-82, and the NIS2 Directive establish specific requirements for risk management in industrial infrastructures. Complying with these standards not only improves the security of the organization, but also facilitates cooperation with regulatory bodies and customers who require assurances on the protection of the infrastructure. Conducting security audits and documenting procedures can demonstrate compliance with these regulations and improve incident preparedness.

The human factor remains one of the biggest vulnerabilities in protecting critical assets. Social engineering attacks, such as phishing, have been used to obtain access credentials to sensitive systems or trick employees into executing malicious commands. Training staff in cybersecurity and raising awareness of common threats can reduce the likelihood of a successful attack. Implementing cyberattack simulations and conducting incident response exercises improves the readiness of operational teams and strengthens the organization's resilience to targeted attacks.

Integrating threat intelligence into critical asset security enables anticipation of targeted attacks. Gathering and analyzing information on emerging threats, malicious actors, and vulnerabilities exploited in other sectors facilitates the implementation of more effective defense strategies. Collaboration with government agencies and industry associations enables sharing information on security incidents and strengthening the resilience of critical infrastructure.

Identifying and protecting critical assets requires a combination of technical measures, continuous monitoring, staff training and regulatory compliance. The increasing interconnectivity of these systems has increased exposure to cyberattacks, making it essential to implement protection strategies tailored to industrial environments. Network segmentation, anomaly detection, access restriction and real-time monitoring can minimize risks and ensure the stability and reliability of industrial systems.

Defense in Depth Strategies for OT

Defense in depth is a security approach that seeks to protect critical infrastructure by implementing multiple layers of protection across network, system, and device levels. In operational technology environments, where system availability is a priority, this approach is essential to mitigate the risks associated with cyberattacks and security breaches. The increasing interconnection between operational technology and information technology has expanded the attack surface, making a security strategy based on a single line of defense insufficient.

One of the fundamental principles of defense in depth is network segmentation. In many industrial environments, control systems are connected to administrative networks or even accessible from the Internet, which increases the risk of exposure to attacks. Segmentation using the zone and pipe model, established in the IEC 62443 standard, allows industrial networks to be isolated and strict access controls to be established between the different segments. Implementing industrial firewalls and configuring demilitarized networks can reduce the exposure of critical devices and prevent lateral movement of attackers within the infrastructure.

Access control is another key layer of defense in depth in OT environments. In many industrial systems, devices still operate with default credentials or access settings without strong authentication. Implementing multi-factor authentication for remote access and centralized credential management minimizes the risk of unauthorized access. Additionally, using role-based access control allows each user to have only the privileges necessary to perform their duties, reducing the possibility that compromised credentials can be used to gain access to sensitive systems.

Real-time threat monitoring and detection are essential elements of a defense-in-depth strategy. Monitoring network traffic and analyzing device behavior can identify anomalous activity patterns that could indicate an intrusion attempt. Implementing intrusion detection systems specifically designed for industrial environments can detect attacks without disrupting operational processes. Correlating events at different levels of the infrastructure makes it easier to identify emerging threats and enables a faster and more effective response to security incidents.

Security on industrial devices is a critical layer in a defense-in-depth strategy. Many programmable logic controllers and SCADA devices have been designed without considering advanced security measures, making them vulnerable to tampering and denial-of-service attacks. Hardening these devices, including removing unnecessary services, restricting access, and applying security updates, helps reduce the attack surface. Additionally, adopting application whitelisting prevents unauthorized software from running on these devices, limiting the possibility of targeted attacks.

Data and communications encryption is another critical layer within defense in depth. Many industrial systems still use unencrypted protocols, allowing attackers to intercept and manipulate information transmitted between devices. Adopting secure protocols such as OPC UA with TLS encryption and implementing digital signatures ensures data integrity and confidentiality. Additionally, the use of hardware security modules makes it possible to protect cryptographic keys used in authentication and encryption of communications.

Control of physical devices within the industrial infrastructure is another key aspect of defence in depth. Attackers may attempt to compromise security by physically accessing servers, control stations or network devices. Implementing physical access controls, including the use of electronic locks, video surveillance and biometric authentication, minimises the risk of direct manipulation of systems. In addition, restricting the use of removable media, such as USB sticks and external drives, helps prevent the introduction of malware into the industrial network.

Resilience to attacks is an essential component of a defense-in-depth strategy. Implementing redundancy in critical systems ensures operational continuity even in the event of a security incident. Performing regular backups and storing them in isolated environments ensures the possibility of recovery from ransomware attacks or other destructive threats. Performing recovery testing and planning business continuity strategies strengthens the organization's ability to respond to serious incidents.

Regulatory compliance is another key factor in defense in depth in OT environments. Standards such as IEC 62443 and NIST 800-82 establish specific guidelines for implementing multiple layers of security in industrial systems. Compliance with these standards improves the security posture of the organization and facilitates cooperation with regulatory bodies and business partners. Conducting security audits and documenting procedures allows the effectiveness of the implemented measures to be evaluated and the defense strategy to be continuously optimized.

Cybersecurity training for staff is an essential layer within defence in depth. Social engineering attacks, such as phishing, remain one of the main threats to industrial systems. Training operators, engineers and administrators in good security practices reduces the likelihood that a successful attack is due to human error. Conducting cyberattack simulations and incident response exercises improves the ability to react to crisis situations and strengthens the security culture within the organisation.

Integrating threat intelligence into your defense-in-depth strategy helps you anticipate targeted attacks and adapt security measures based on emerging risks. Gathering and analyzing cyber threat intelligence makes it easier to detect attack patterns and implement automated responses. Collaboration with government agencies, industry associations, and intelligence-sharing platforms strengthens your infrastructure's defense capabilities and enables a more coordinated response to large-scale threats.

Defense in depth in OT environments requires a holistic approach that combines network segmentation, access control, threat monitoring, communications encryption, and staff training. The increasing interconnectivity of industrial systems has increased exposure to cyberattacks, making it essential to implement multiple layers of security that reduce the attack surface and ensure operational continuity. Adoption of advanced technologies, regulatory compliance, and integration of threat intelligence strengthen the resilience of critical infrastructures and enable effective addressing of cybersecurity challenges in operational technology.

Cloud Security for Industrial Systems

The adoption of cloud computing in industrial environments has enabled improved operational efficiency, optimized data analysis, and facilitated remote access to monitoring and control systems. The integration of cloud services with operational technology infrastructures has enabled the implementation of advanced solutions based on artificial intelligence, predictive maintenance, and real-time analysis. However, this transformation has also introduced new security risks that must be properly managed to prevent the exposure of critical systems to cyberattacks.

One of the main challenges in cloud security for industrial systems is the protection of data transmitted between field devices and cloud platforms. Interconnecting sensors, programmable logic controllers and SCADA systems with cloud data storage and analysis services requires the use of robust encryption mechanisms that guarantee the integrity and confidentiality of information. Adopting secure protocols such as MQTT with TLS and OPC UA with end-to-end encryption helps reduce the possibility of data interception and manipulation attacks during transmission.

Access to cloud platforms from industrial systems must be controlled through strict authentication and authorization policies. In many environments, devices and users access cloud services with shared credentials or overly permissive access settings, making it easy to exploit compromised credentials. Implementing multi-factor authentication, role-based identity management, and segmenting permissions by access level minimizes the risk of unauthorized access to cloud infrastructure.

Continuous monitoring of cloud activity is a key strategy for detecting threats and preventing security incidents in industrial environments. Implementing cloud-based security solutions, such as anomaly detection and security event monitoring (SIEM) tools, can identify suspicious activity patterns and generate real-time alerts in the event of unauthorized access attempts or unexpected changes to system configurations. Correlating events between cloud infrastructure and industrial control systems facilitates the detection of advanced threats and improves incident response capabilities.

Network segmentation in cloud infrastructure is a critical measure to protect industrial systems from unauthorized access. In many deployments, cloud services are directly connected to control devices without proper restrictions, allowing a vulnerability in the cloud to be used as an entry point to attack industrial infrastructure. Creating isolated environments using virtual networks, implementing cloud firewalls, and using access control lists can minimize the exposure of critical devices and reduce the attack surface.

Compliance in the adoption of cloud solutions for industrial environments is a key aspect in security management. Regulations such as IEC 62443 and the NIST cybersecurity framework establish specific requirements for the protection of critical infrastructures, including access management, data encryption and network segmentation. Complying with these standards ensures the security of information stored in the cloud, reduces exposure to attacks and improves the ability to respond to security incidents. Conducting security audits and documenting configurations allows the effectiveness of the measures implemented to be evaluated and the cloud protection strategy to be continuously optimized.

Using artificial intelligence in cloud security for industrial systems enables improved threat detection and incident response automation. Integrating machine learning models into security monitoring solutions makes it easier to identify attack patterns and proactively mitigate risks before they can impact operations. Additionally, automating security policies through configuration management and access control tools reduces the possibility of human error and ensures that protective measures are applied uniformly across the entire cloud infrastructure.

Cloud infrastructure resilience is a critical aspect of ensuring operational continuity in industrial environments. Adopting redundancy strategies, replicating data across multiple regions, and implementing disaster recovery plans can minimize the impact of security incidents or infrastructure failures. Conducting regular recovery tests and validating cloud-stored backups ensures that critical information can be quickly restored in the event of a ransomware attack or other destructive incident.

The human factor remains one of the biggest vulnerabilities in cloud security for industrial systems. Social engineering attacks, such as phishing, have been used to compromise credentials for accessing cloud platforms and gain access to control systems. Training staff in good cybersecurity practices and raising awareness of common threats can reduce the likelihood of a successful attack. Implementing cyberattack simulations and conducting incident response exercises improves the preparedness of operational teams and strengthens the organization's resilience to targeted attacks.

Integrating threat intelligence into cloud security for industrial systems enables anticipation of targeted attacks and adaptation of defense strategies based on emerging risks. Gathering and analyzing cyber threat intelligence facilitates the detection of attack patterns and the implementation of automated responses. Collaboration with government agencies, industry associations, and intelligence-sharing platforms strengthens the infrastructure's defense capabilities and enables a more coordinated response to large-scale threats.

Cloud security for industrial systems requires a comprehensive approach that combines data encryption, access management, continuous monitoring, and regulatory compliance. The increasing interconnectivity of industrial systems with cloud platforms has increased exposure to cyberattacks, making it essential to implement multiple layers of protection that reduce the attack surface and ensure operational continuity. Adopting advanced technologies, complying with security standards, and integrating threat intelligence strengthen the resilience of industrial infrastructures and enable them to effectively address cybersecurity challenges in connected environments.

Security Incident Management in OT: Real Cases

Security incident management in operational technology is a fundamental process to ensure the continuity of industrial operations and minimize the impact of cyber attacks. Over the past few years, numerous incidents have been recorded in OT environments affecting production, energy supply, transportation, and other strategic sectors. The complexity of these attacks and the difficulty in responding to them have demonstrated the importance of having structured procedures for detection, containment, and recovery. Analyzing real cases allows us to understand the challenges and best practices in incident management in OT.

One of the most significant attacks in the history of industrial cybersecurity was the case of Stuxnet, a highly sophisticated malware that was designed to sabotage Iran's nuclear program. This computer worm managed to infiltrate SCADA systems used to control centrifuges at uranium enrichment facilities. Through the manipulation of programmable logic controllers, the malware altered the operation of centrifuges without triggering alarms in monitoring systems. The late detection of this attack highlighted the importance of continuous monitoring and network segmentation to prevent the spread of threats in critical infrastructures.

Another significant incident occurred in 2015 in Ukraine, where a cyberattack targeting the power grid left more than 200,000 people without power. The attackers gained access to the remote control systems of electrical substations using phishing techniques targeting employees. Once inside the network, the attackers took control of the distribution switches and disconnected several substations simultaneously. They also sabotaged the SCADA systems, preventing operators from being able to restore service quickly. This case demonstrated the need to restrict remote access and reinforce staff training in identifying malicious emails.

In 2021, the attack on the Colonial Pipeline in the United States highlighted the vulnerability of the energy industry to ransomware. A group of cybercriminals managed to compromise the company's IT network, blocking access to administrative systems essential to the operation of the pipeline. Although the OT systems were not directly affected, the company made the decision to stop the supply of fuel as a preventive measure. This generated a crisis in the distribution of gasoline and diesel on the east coast of the United States. The attack highlighted the importance of segmentation between IT and OT networks, as well as the need to have specific incident response plans for ransomware attacks.

In the water and wastewater sector, an alarming case occurred in 2021 in Florida, where an attacker managed to remotely access the Oldsmar water treatment plant. Through a remote desktop connection without multi-factor authentication, the attacker attempted to modify the sodium hydroxide levels in the drinking water, increasing its concentration to dangerous levels. Fortunately, an operator detected the suspicious activity and reversed the changes before the contaminated water reached consumers. This incident highlighted the importance of restricting remote access to critical infrastructure and implementing real-time monitoring to detect unauthorized modifications to control systems.

Incident response in OT must be fast and coordinated to minimize damage. One of the main challenges is that in many cases, IT and OT security teams work separately, making it difficult to efficiently manage a crisis. In one incident recorded at a manufacturing plant in 2019, unknown malware infected workstations used for monitoring production lines. Due to a lack of communication between IT and OT teams, the infection spread for several hours before being contained. During this time, industrial operators attempted to resolve the issue by rebooting affected systems without understanding the scope of the attack. This led to production losses and extended downtime.

Best practices in OT incident management include implementing specific response procedures for industrial environments. Early detection of anomalies is a key aspect, as many OT attacks do not generate immediate alerts. Integrating AI-based monitoring tools makes it possible to identify changes in the behavior of control devices and detect suspicious activities before they become critical incidents.

Isolating compromised devices is an effective strategy to contain the spread of an attack. In an incident at a refinery in 2020, operators were able to prevent a larger attack by physically disconnecting a segment of the network that had been compromised by malware. This action prevented attackers from accessing SCADA systems and minimized the impact of the incident. The ability to respond quickly was due to the existence of a well-defined contingency plan and the training of staff in the execution of emergency measures.

System recovery after an OT incident is a complex process that must ensure the safe restoration of operations. In a documented case at an automotive assembly plant in 2018, a ransomware attack affected production servers and devices connected to the industrial network. The company had backups in place, but restoration was complicated by the lack of specific procedures for control systems. Manual reconfiguration of PLCs and validation of systems delayed recovery for several days. This case highlighted the need for regular recovery testing and ensuring that backups included OT-specific settings and parameters.

The evolution of cyber threats in industrial environments has shown that incident management in OT cannot rely solely on traditional IT security approaches. The combination of continuous monitoring, network segmentation, strict authentication and staff training is essential to reduce risks and improve the ability to respond to cyber attacks. Analyzing real-life attack cases allows us to identify lessons learned and adapt security strategies to meet the challenges of an increasingly digitalized and interconnected environment.

Security in Wireless Communication Systems in OT

Wireless communication systems in operational technology have enabled greater flexibility and efficiency in industrial process management, facilitating the interconnection of devices without the need for complex wiring infrastructures. Sensors, programmable logic controllers and SCADA systems have adopted technologies such as Wi-Fi, Bluetooth, Zigbee and cellular networks for remote monitoring and control of operations in industrial environments. However, the implementation of these technologies has also increased the attack surface, introducing new security risks that must be mitigated to prevent tampering with critical systems and disruption of essential operations.

One of the main challenges in securing wireless communications in OT is the lack of adequate encryption in many deployments. In many industrial environments, connections between sensors and control systems still use unencrypted protocols or outdated security mechanisms, allowing an attacker to intercept and manipulate transmitted data through man-in-the-middle (MITM) attacks. Adopting advanced encryption standards, such as WPA3 in Wi-Fi networks and AES-256 in industrial communication links, is critical to protecting the integrity and confidentiality of transmitted data.

Unauthorized access to wireless networks is another major risk in OT. Many industrial deployments allow wireless connections without adequate restrictions, making it easy for attackers to connect to the network and probe internal systems for vulnerabilities. Implementing strong authentication through digital certificates, access control lists (ACLs), and network segmentation reduces the risk of unauthorized access. Additionally, using hidden networks and restricting connections to specific devices minimizes the possibility of targeted attacks against the wireless infrastructure.

Interference and denial-of-service attacks pose a significant threat to wireless communication systems in OT. In industrial environments, wireless signals can be intentionally disrupted through the use of jamming equipment or attacks, affecting the connectivity of critical sensors and devices. Implementing interference detection mechanisms and using redundant frequencies can minimize the impact of these attacks. Furthermore, the use of technologies such as Frequency Hopping Spread Spectrum (FHSS) and Direct Sequence Spread Spectrum (DSSS) reduces the vulnerability of industrial networks to deliberate interference attempts.

Monitoring and detecting anomalies in wireless networks is essential for OT security. Real-time monitoring of network traffic allows for the identification of suspicious access attempts, variations in signal strength, and anomalous behavior in data transmission. Integrating wireless-specific intrusion detection tools makes it easier to identify unknown devices and generate alerts in the event of potential attacks. Correlating events between wired and wireless networks improves incident response capabilities and enables more effective threat mitigation.

Wireless network segmentation in industrial environments is a key strategy to minimize security risks. Separating critical devices from corporate and public access networks prevents an attacker from using insecure connections to infiltrate control systems. Implementing specific VLANs for industrial traffic and restricting communication between network segments reduces the possibility of lateral movement within the infrastructure. Additionally, the use of industrial firewalls and wireless security gateways allows for the establishment of advanced filtering and monitoring rules to protect the infrastructure from unauthorized access.

IoT and IIoT devices operating over wireless networks in OT represent an emerging attack vector. Many low-power devices used in industrial automation lack adequate security mechanisms, allowing them to be exploited for privilege escalation or denial of service attacks. Implementing certificate-based authentication, restricting communication traffic, and continuously monitoring these devices minimizes the risk of vulnerability exploitation. Furthermore, adopting Zero Trust architectures in IoT device management ensures that only authenticated and authorized devices can communicate with industrial systems.

The use of cellular networks in OT, such as 4G and 5G, has enabled more stable and secure connectivity in remote industrial environments. However, these technologies also present specific risks related to data manipulation and communications interception. Implementing encrypted VPN tunnels on cellular connections and using SIM-based authentication reduce the risk of traffic interception. Furthermore, adopting virtual private networks (industrial VPNs) in critical infrastructures ensures that communications between mobile devices and control systems are secure and protected against external attacks.

Regulatory compliance in wireless communications security in OT is a fundamental aspect in the protection of industrial infrastructures. Regulations such as IEC 62443 and the NIST Cybersecurity Framework establish specific requirements for the protection of industrial networks and connected devices. Compliance with these standards allows for improved wireless communications security, reduced exposure to attacks, and facilitates the integration of best practices in the management of critical infrastructures. Implementing security audits and performing penetration tests on wireless networks allows for the evaluation of the effectiveness of the implemented measures and the continuous optimization of the security strategy.

The human factor remains one of the biggest vulnerabilities in the security of wireless communication systems in OT. Social engineering attacks, such as phishing and the use of rogue APs, have been used to trick employees into gaining access credentials to industrial networks. Training staff in good cybersecurity practices and raising awareness of common threats can reduce the likelihood of a successful attack. Implementing wireless attack simulations and conducting incident response exercises strengthens the readiness of operational teams and improves threat detection capabilities.

Security in wireless communication systems in OT requires a combination of technical strategies, continuous monitoring, network segmentation and regulatory compliance. The increasing interconnectivity of industrial devices has increased exposure to cyberattacks, making it essential to implement protection measures adapted to wireless environments. Network segmentation, communications encryption, robust authentication and real-time monitoring help minimize risks and ensure the stability and reliability of industrial systems that rely on wireless technologies for their operation.

The Role of Artificial Intelligence in Industrial Cybersecurity

Artificial intelligence has transformed the approach to cybersecurity in industrial environments, allowing threats to be detected more quickly and accurately compared to traditional methods. The increasing digitalization of operational technology has increased the complexity of security in critical infrastructures, making it necessary to use intelligent systems that can analyze large volumes of data and respond autonomously to potential attacks. The integration of artificial intelligence in industrial cybersecurity has improved anomaly detection, incident management, and device protection in automation networks.

One of the key benefits of AI in industrial cybersecurity is its ability to detect threats in real time. Unlike traditional methods based on malware signatures or lists of known threats, AI models can identify anomalous behavior in systems without prior knowledge of a specific threat. This capability is especially useful in OT environments, where devices and communication protocols vary widely and where attacks can take new and sophisticated forms.

AI-based behavioral analysis is one of the most valuable applications in industrial cybersecurity. By continuously monitoring activity on networks, devices, and control systems, machine learning algorithms can establish a baseline of normal operation and detect deviations that could indicate an attack in progress. For example, if a programmable logic controller starts receiving unusual commands at an unusual time, the AI system can generate an alert and trigger response mechanisms before significant damage is done.

AI-powered autonomous response systems have improved the ability to react to cybersecurity incidents in industrial environments. In many organizations, the detection of an attack relies on human intervention, which can lead to delays in threat mitigation. AI makes it possible to automate incident response by applying predefined rules and analyzing security events in real time. If a system detects suspicious traffic coming from an unauthorized IP address, it can automatically block the connection and notify security teams without the need for manual intervention.

Artificial intelligence has also strengthened security in authentication and access management in industrial environments. The adoption of facial recognition models, advanced biometrics and analysis of usage patterns has made it possible to improve user identification and prevent unauthorized access. In industrial plants where multiple employees and suppliers access control systems, artificial intelligence can detect unusual access attempts and apply adaptive security measures based on the level of risk detected.

In the field of malware and ransomware detection, artificial intelligence has proven to be more effective than traditional approaches. Instead of relying on previously identified threat signatures, machine learning-based systems analyze the behavior of running software to identify malicious patterns. This makes it possible to detect new malware variants that have not yet been cataloged by conventional security solutions. In industrial environments, where a ransomware attack can paralyze production and cause multimillion-dollar losses, proactive detection based on artificial intelligence is a key tool for protecting infrastructure.

Artificial intelligence has also emerged as an ally in vulnerability management in industrial systems. Identifying and mitigating security flaws in OT devices is a challenge, as many of these systems cannot be updated as frequently as IT devices. By analyzing global security data, AI can predict which vulnerabilities are most likely to be exploited and recommend mitigation measures before they are exploited by attackers. This capability allows organizations to prioritize the remediation of critical vulnerabilities and reduce exposure to unnecessary risks.

The use of artificial intelligence in security event correlation has improved the ability of response teams to identify complex attacks on industrial infrastructures. Attacks targeting control systems can involve multiple attack vectors, such as unauthorized access, data manipulation, and denial of service. Artificial intelligence can analyze thousands of events in real time, identify attack patterns, and provide an integrated view of the ongoing threat. This facilitates decision-making and enables a more effective response to security incidents.

Despite its advantages, the implementation of AI in industrial cybersecurity also faces challenges. The quality and quantity of data used to train AI models directly affect their accuracy and effectiveness. If an AI system does not have enough data representative of the normal operation of an industrial infrastructure, it could generate false positives or fail to detect real threats. Furthermore, attackers have begun to develop evasion techniques designed to fool detection algorithms, making constant monitoring and updating of AI models used in industrial security necessary.

Compliance and regulation of the use of artificial intelligence in industrial cybersecurity is also a key aspect to consider. Standards such as IEC 62443 establish guidelines for security in operational technology, and their integration with artificial intelligence solutions must ensure transparency in decision-making of security models. The adoption of artificial intelligence in industrial environments must be aligned with regulations and best practices to ensure the protection of systems without affecting the availability and stability of the operation.

Combining AI with traditional cybersecurity strategies has proven to be one of the most effective ways to protect industrial infrastructures against advanced threats. Integrating AI solutions into monitoring, authentication, malware detection, and behavioral analysis systems has made it possible to improve organizations' resilience against cyberattacks. As threats evolve and become more sophisticated, AI will continue to play a key role in protecting operational technology and ensuring operational continuity in industrial environments.

Data Protection in Critical Infrastructures

Data protection in critical infrastructures is a fundamental aspect of industrial cybersecurity, as these infrastructures depend on the integrity, availability and confidentiality of information to operate safely and efficiently. Sectors such as energy, transportation, water and sanitation, telecommunications and manufacturing depend on accurate data for decision-making and process control. A compromise in data integrity can lead to operational failures, interruptions in the provision of essential services and even risks to public safety.

One of the main challenges in data protection in critical infrastructures is the increasing interconnectivity of industrial systems with IT networks and cloud computing. The digitalization of processes has enabled improved operational efficiency, but it has also increased the attack surface. Data transmission between control systems, sensors and analysis platforms must be protected against unauthorized access, malicious manipulation and interception attacks. The implementation of robust encryption protocols, such as TLS for data transmission and AES-256 for storage, is one of the essential measures to ensure the confidentiality and integrity of information.

Access to data in critical infrastructures must be restricted to authorized users and systems through authentication and identity management controls. In many industrial environments, devices and users share credentials or use weak passwords, making it easy to exploit compromised access. Adopting multi-factor authentication, centralized identity management, and role-based access control minimizes the possibility of unauthorized access. In addition, continuous access auditing and the implementation of activity logs make it possible to detect suspicious access attempts and respond to potential threats.

Secure data storage in critical infrastructures is another key aspect of data protection. Many organizations rely on databases and storage servers that can become targets for ransomware attacks or data exfiltration. Implementing segmentation measures in storage environments, restricting administrative access, and using anomaly detection systems when handling data helps prevent data theft or alteration. Additionally, using encrypted backups stored in isolated environments ensures recovery in the event of an attack or system failure.

Ransomware attacks have posed a growing threat to data protection in critical infrastructures. In recent years, there have been incidents in which essential service operators have been affected by malware that encrypts critical data and demands payment for its recovery. Implementing ransomware protection strategies, such as segmenting sensitive data, restricting access with high privileges and adopting early detection solutions, is essential to minimize the impact of these attacks. Regular recovery testing from backups allows the effectiveness of protection strategies to be evaluated and operational continuity to be guaranteed.

Real-time monitoring and supervision of data transmitted and stored in critical infrastructures allows for the detection of manipulation attempts before they affect operations. The integration of monitoring tools based on artificial intelligence facilitates the identification of unusual patterns in data access, configuration modifications and the transmission of information outside normal operating limits. The correlation of events between multiple security systems allows for improved incident response capacity and reduced detection time for potential attacks.

Compliance with data protection regulations in critical infrastructures is a fundamental aspect of ensuring information security. Regulations such as IEC 62443, the NIST Cybersecurity Framework, and the NIS2 Directive establish specific requirements for data protection in strategic sectors. Compliance with these regulations not only improves the security of the infrastructure, but also facilitates cooperation with regulatory bodies and clients that require guarantees on the protection of information. Conducting security audits and documenting procedures allows the effectiveness of the implemented measures to be evaluated and the data protection strategy to be continuously improved.

The human factor remains one of the main vulnerabilities in data protection in critical infrastructures. Social engineering attacks, such as phishing and identity theft, have been used to obtain access credentials to data storage systems and manipulate critical information. Training staff in good cybersecurity practices and raising awareness of the most common threats can reduce the likelihood of an attack being successful. Implementing cyberattack simulations and conducting incident response exercises reinforces the preparation of operational teams and improves the organization's resilience to targeted attacks.

Network segmentation and traffic restriction between storage systems and control devices are effective strategies for reducing data exposure to cyberattacks. In many industrial environments, data servers share infrastructure with control systems, allowing an attacker who compromises one part of the network to access sensitive information. Implementing industrial firewalls, application whitelists, and strict access controls minimizes the possibility of data being accessed or manipulated without authorization.

Adopting threat intelligence to protect critical infrastructure data enables anticipation of targeted attacks and adaptation of security strategies based on emerging risks. Gathering and analyzing cyber threat intelligence facilitates the detection of attack patterns and the implementation of automated responses. Collaboration with government agencies, industry associations, and intelligence-sharing platforms strengthens the infrastructure's defense capabilities and enables a more coordinated response to large-scale threats.

Data protection in critical infrastructures requires a combination of encryption strategies, access management, continuous monitoring, network segmentation and regulatory compliance. Growing digitalisation and interconnectivity have increased the exposure of data to cyberattacks, making it essential to implement security measures adapted to industrial environments. The integration of advanced technologies, staff training and the adoption of good practices in data management make it possible to guarantee the integrity, confidentiality and availability of information in critical infrastructures, ensuring operational continuity and reducing the risks associated with the manipulation or loss of essential data.

Security in Industrial Software Development

Industrial software development is a critical component in the automation and control of essential infrastructures such as manufacturing plants, power grids, transportation systems, and water management. As these systems are modernized and integrated with new technologies, cybersecurity becomes a determining factor in ensuring their reliability, integrity, and availability. A security error in the code of industrial control software can generate vulnerabilities that can be exploited by attackers, affecting the operation of critical processes and compromising the security of facilities.

One of the biggest challenges in industrial software development is the coexistence of legacy technologies with new digital platforms. Many industrial systems have been designed without considering cybersecurity as a fundamental requirement, resulting in applications with insecure default configurations, default credentials, and a lack of encryption mechanisms. As these platforms are updated and connected to external networks, existing vulnerabilities can be exploited by attackers. The "security by design" approach has become essential in industrial software development, ensuring that security is an integral part of the development lifecycle and not an afterthought.

Source code management in industrial software must include robust security practices to prevent the introduction of vulnerabilities during development. Code review, the use of static analysis tools, and the implementation of automated security testing enable errors to be detected before applications are deployed in production environments. Adopting secure development methodologies, such as Microsoft's SDL (Security Development Lifecycle) model, ensures that security is assessed at every stage of the process, from initial design to implementation and maintenance.

Access control and authentication in industrial applications are critical aspects of their security. Many industrial software systems still allow access without strong authentication or use shared credentials among multiple users. This increases the risk of unauthorized access and facilitates the exploitation of compromised credentials. Implementing multi-factor authentication, using role-based authorization mechanisms, and eliminating default accounts improves software security and reduces the possibility of unauthorized access to control systems.

Data encryption in industrial software is a key measure to ensure the protection of transmitted and stored information. Many communication protocols used in industry still operate without encryption, allowing attackers to intercept and manipulate critical data. The adoption of advanced encryption standards, such as TLS for data transmission and AES-256 for storage, reduces the risk of interception and guarantees the integrity of information. In addition, the use of digital signatures in the distribution of software updates ensures that the installed versions are legitimate and have not been altered by attackers.

Network segmentation is another essential strategy in industrial software security. In many environments, control and monitoring applications are connected to corporate networks or exposed to the Internet without adequate restrictions. This makes it easier for an attacker to exploit a vulnerability in the software to access other systems within the infrastructure. Implementing firewalls, demilitarized networks, and strict access controls limits the software's exposure to external threats and prevents lateral movement within the network in the event of an intrusion.

Penetration testing in industrial software allows the security of applications to be assessed before they are deployed. These tests simulate real attacks to identify vulnerabilities and correct them before they can be exploited. In industrial software development, testing must be carried out in controlled environments that do not affect the operation of production systems. The combination of manual and automated testing allows both configuration errors and vulnerabilities in the code to be detected.

Regulatory compliance is a key factor in the security of industrial software development. Standards such as IEC 62443 and the NIST framework establish specific requirements for the protection of industrial control systems and applications. Complying with these regulations ensures that the software developed follows security best practices and minimizes the risks associated with its use in critical infrastructure. Documenting secure development processes and performing security audits can demonstrate compliance with these standards and improve application resilience against cyberattacks.

Maintaining and updating industrial software is a critical aspect of its security. Many successful attacks occur due to the exploitation of vulnerabilities in outdated, unpatched versions of software. Update management must be done in a planned manner to avoid operational disruptions, ensuring that new versions are compatible with existing infrastructure. Implementing secure update distribution mechanisms, such as digital signature and integrity verification, prevents the installation of malicious software that may have been tampered with during the distribution process.

The human factor remains one of the main vulnerabilities in industrial software development security. Coding errors, incorrect permission settings, and lack of data entry validations can create points of exploitation for attackers. Continuous training of developers in good security practices and fostering a secure development culture are essential to reduce these risks. Conducting security workshops and integrating security testing into the development process improves software quality and reduces the possibility of critical errors.

Artificial intelligence and machine learning have begun to play an important role in industrial software security. Advanced code analysis tools can detect patterns of vulnerabilities and recommend solutions before the software is deployed in production. In addition, artificial intelligence can be used in monitoring systems to detect anomalies in the operation of the software and alert about possible attempts at manipulation or attacks.

Secure industrial software development requires a comprehensive approach that combines secure development methodologies, robust authentication, data encryption, security testing, and regulatory compliance. The increasing digitalization of industrial systems has increased exposure to cyberattacks, making it essential to adopt security strategies at every stage of development. Implementing appropriate controls, continuous software updates, and staff training can reduce risks and ensure that industrial applications are protected from cyber threats.

OT Cybersecurity Maturity Assessment

OT cybersecurity maturity assessment is a fundamental process to measure the level of protection of industrial infrastructures and determine an organization's capabilities to face cyber threats. Given the growth of cyberattacks targeting operational technology environments, organizations must implement structured frameworks to identify vulnerabilities, establish security controls, and improve their resilience to incidents. Unlike information technology environments, where security strategies are more advanced, in OT security must be balanced with availability and operational continuity.

One of the most widely used models for OT cybersecurity maturity assessment is the National Institute of Standards and Technology (NIST) framework, which defines five key functions: identify, protect, detect, respond, and recover. This structure allows organizations to assess their security capabilities in each area and establish a roadmap for continuous improvement. The identify phase focuses on understanding critical infrastructure assets, their risks, and potential threats. The protect phase assesses the controls in place to reduce exposure to attacks. Detection measures the organization's ability to identify anomalous activities and potential security incidents. Response looks at the procedures in place to mitigate an ongoing attack. Recovery examines the system's resilience and its ability to restore operation following an incident.

Another widely adopted framework in OT maturity assessment is the IEC 62443 standard, which provides a structured approach to security in industrial control systems. This standard allows for assessing the security level of an infrastructure by identifying zones and conduits, implementing network segmentation measures, and enforcing access control policies. An organization's IEC 62443 maturity is measured at levels ranging from an initial state of minimal security to an advanced level where cybersecurity is fully integrated into the operation.

OT cybersecurity maturity assessment requires the application of diagnostic tools that allow measuring the current state of security in industrial infrastructure. Security audits are one of the most widely used methodologies to assess OT maturity, as they allow the analysis of network configurations, access policies, software updates and regulatory compliance. In addition, penetration tests specific to industrial environments facilitate the identification of vulnerabilities that could be exploited by attackers.

Continuous monitoring is a key indicator in assessing OT cybersecurity maturity. An organization with a low level of cybersecurity maturity often relies on manual controls and lacks real-time visibility into security events in its infrastructure. As cybersecurity maturity increases, organizations deploy intrusion detection systems, AI-based monitoring, and behavioral analytics to identify threats before they impact operations. The ability to correlate security events across multiple levels of the infrastructure is a sign of a high degree of OT maturity.

Access control is another critical aspect in the OT cybersecurity maturity assessment. Many industrial organizations still use shared credentials, default accounts, and weak authentication mechanisms, making them vulnerable to unauthorized access. A low maturity level in this aspect indicates a lack of robust authentication policies and centralized identity management. As the organization progresses in maturity, it implements multifactor authentication, role-based access segmentation, and continuous session monitoring to detect intrusion attempts.

Vulnerability management is a key factor in OT cybersecurity maturity. In many industrial infrastructures, systems operate on legacy software that does not receive frequent security updates. A low maturity level is reflected in the lack of a patch management program and the exposure of critical devices to known vulnerabilities. Organizations with a high maturity level implement mitigation strategies to protect non-updatable systems, such as network segmentation, application whitelisting, and integrity monitoring on industrial devices.

The human factor is a critical aspect in assessing OT cybersecurity maturity. In low-maturity environments, cybersecurity awareness among system operators and administrators is limited, increasing the risk of human error and social engineering attacks. As the organization matures, industrial cybersecurity training programs, attack simulations, and incident response exercises are established. Organizations with an advanced level of maturity embed cybersecurity into the operational culture and ensure that each employee understands their role in protecting the infrastructure.

Incident response capability is an essential metric in OT maturity assessment. Organizations with a low maturity level lack structured response plans and rely on reactive actions when a threat is detected. At an intermediate maturity level, organizations develop documented response procedures, establish incident response teams, and conduct recovery testing to minimize the impact of attacks. At the highest maturity level, organizations automate incident response using advanced tools and collaborate with other industry players to share threat intelligence and improve their defense capabilities.

Regulatory compliance is a determining factor in the OT cybersecurity maturity assessment. An organization with a low maturity level does not have policies aligned with international regulations and lacks security audits. As maturity increases, the organization establishes processes to comply with regulations such as IEC 62443, NIST 800-82, and the NIS2 Directive. Organizations with an advanced level of OT cybersecurity maturity not only comply with regulations, but also implement continuous improvements to their security strategies based on evolving threats.

The OT cybersecurity maturity assessment is a continuous process that allows organizations to measure their current status, identify areas for improvement, and establish a strategy to strengthen the security of their industrial infrastructures. The combination of advanced monitoring, access control, vulnerability management, staff training, and regulatory compliance allows organizations to achieve a high level of maturity and ensure the resilience of their systems against cyber threats.

Industrial Safety Training and Awareness

Industrial security training and awareness are key elements to strengthen the protection of critical infrastructure and operational technology systems. As digitalization and automation advance in industrial environments, the risks of cyberattacks increase, and the lack of preparation of personnel can become one of the greatest vulnerabilities. Threats come not only from external malicious actors, but also from human errors, improper configurations and poor operational practices that can compromise the security of systems.

One of the challenges in industrial security training is the lack of a cybersecurity culture in OT environments. For decades, security in industry has focused on physical aspects, such as preventing workplace accidents and protecting equipment, leaving digital security in the background. Many operators, engineers and technicians have not received specific cybersecurity training, making them more prone to making mistakes that can be exploited by attackers. Implementing structured training programs is critical to ensuring that all employees understand their role in protecting industrial infrastructure.

Industrial security training should be tailored to different roles within the organization. Plant operators, network administrators, software developers, and maintenance personnel all have different responsibilities and therefore require specific training based on their activities. Operators must learn to identify suspicious activity in control systems, while network administrators need to know best practices in segmenting and protecting industrial networks. Customizing training ensures that each worker receives knowledge relevant to their role within the organization.

One of the most critical aspects of industrial security awareness is the prevention of social engineering attacks. Many successful cyberattacks begin with psychological manipulation techniques, such as phishing emails, fraudulent phone calls, and messages that attempt to trick employees into revealing credentials or running malicious files. Training in this area should include practical exercises where employees can learn to identify deception attempts, verify the authenticity of messages, and apply appropriate security measures before interacting with suspicious emails or links.

Cyberattack simulations are an effective tool to strengthen staff preparedness for security incidents. Incident response exercises allow employees to assess their ability to respond to an attack and detect possible flaws in established procedures. Simulations of ransomware, unauthorized access attempts, and denial of service attacks help improve the organization's ability to react and optimize security protocols. In addition, conducting internal audits and controlled penetration tests provides valuable information on areas that require improvements in infrastructure security.

Training in the secure use of industrial devices and control systems is essential to reducing the attack surface in OT environments. Many security incidents are caused by improper configurations on control equipment, lack of updates on devices, and insecure remote access practices. Training should address the importance of using secure credentials, restricting access to critical systems, and applying configurations that minimize the risks of vulnerability exploitation.

Regulatory compliance is another critical aspect of industrial safety training. There are various international regulations and standards, such as IEC 62443, NIST 800-82, and the NIS2 Directive, that set specific requirements for the protection of industrial infrastructure. Employees must be familiar with these regulations and understand how they affect their daily work. Regulatory compliance training ensures that the organization implements best security practices and avoids penalties for non-compliance with applicable regulations.

Constantly updating cybersecurity knowledge is a key component of effective training. Threats continually evolve, and the tactics used by attackers adapt to new technologies. Training should not be a one-time event, but rather an ongoing process in which employees receive up-to-date information on the latest threats, defense strategies, and protection technologies. The organization should foster a culture of lifelong learning in cybersecurity, encouraging participation in specialized courses, certifications, and seminars.

The use of interactive platforms and digital tools facilitates industrial safety training. The implementation of online courses, virtual simulations and gamified training environments allows employees to learn in a dynamic and practical way. The combination of theory and practical exercises improves knowledge retention and allows workers to experience safety scenarios in a safe environment before facing real situations.

Senior management leadership in promoting industrial security is a key determinant of the success of training programs. When organizational leaders prioritize cybersecurity and establish clear policies in this area, employees adopt a more proactive mindset in protecting infrastructure. Security should be a shared responsibility throughout the organization, and not a task exclusively for the IT team or the security department. Cybersecurity awareness should be integrated into the corporate culture so that it becomes a fundamental principle in all operations.

Evaluating the effectiveness of industrial safety training allows you to measure its impact and make adjustments based on the needs of the organization. Applying knowledge tests, conducting safety perception surveys, and analyzing incidents recorded before and after the implementation of training programs help determine the degree of improvement in employee preparedness. Effective training should result in a reduction in the number of human errors related to safety incidents and in increased threat detection capabilities by staff.

Industrial security training and awareness are fundamental aspects of protecting critical infrastructure. The combination of role-specific training, cyberattack simulations, regulatory compliance, and organizational leadership can strengthen security in OT environments and minimize the risks of incidents. The constant evolution of threats makes ongoing training a necessity in industrial cybersecurity, ensuring that employees are prepared to face challenges in an increasingly digitalized and interconnected environment.

Future Trends in OT Cybersecurity

Cybersecurity in operational technology is evolving rapidly due to the rise in threats targeting critical infrastructure and the increasing interconnectivity between industrial systems and corporate networks. Digital transformation in industry has enabled process optimization and improved efficiency, but it has also generated new vulnerabilities that attackers can exploit. Emerging trends in OT cybersecurity seek to address these challenges by adopting advanced technologies, strengthening security controls, and implementing more robust protection strategies.

One of the major changes in OT cybersecurity is the adoption of security architectures based on the Zero Trust model. Traditionally, industrial environments have operated under the principle that systems within the operational technology network are trusted, which has led to more flexible security configurations within the infrastructure. However, recent attacks have shown that attackers can infiltrate the network through compromised credentials or vulnerabilities in connected devices. The Zero Trust approach is based on the premise that no connection is trusted by default, requiring continuous identity checks, traffic monitoring, and strict access segmentation to reduce the attack surface.

Artificial intelligence and machine learning are playing an increasingly important role in threat detection and response in industrial environments. As attacks become more sophisticated and difficult to identify using traditional methods, AI makes it possible to analyse large volumes of data in real time and detect anomalies in the behaviour of devices and networks. AI-based intrusion detection systems can identify unusual patterns in communication between sensors, programmable logic controllers and SCADA systems, allowing for an early response to potential attacks before they compromise the operation.

Cloud security for industrial environments is constantly evolving due to the integration of remote monitoring and data analysis platforms into critical infrastructures. Many organizations have begun to move part of their operations to cloud environments to improve accessibility and centralized data management. However, this also introduces new risks related to the protection of information and the authentication of connected devices. Current trends in cloud security for OT include the implementation of end-to-end encryption in communications, hardware-based authentication to ensure device identity, and the use of hybrid models that allow maintaining control over sensitive data while taking advantage of the benefits of cloud computing.

The Industrial Internet of Things continues to expand in OT environments, with thousands of connected sensors and devices generating real-time information to optimize production and improve energy efficiency. However, the security of these devices remains a critical concern, as many manufacturers fail to include adequate protection measures in their products. The trend towards the adoption of specific security standards for industrial devices seeks to ensure that connected equipment meets minimum protection requirements before being integrated into OT networks. In addition, whitelisting of authorized devices and strict network segmentation can minimize the impact of vulnerabilities on industrial IoT devices.

Cyber threats targeting critical infrastructure have evolved into more sophisticated and persistent attacks. State-sponsored attack groups have demonstrated their ability to compromise operational technology networks through advanced penetration techniques and manipulation of control systems. The future trend in OT cybersecurity includes a more proactive approach to threat intelligence, through collaboration between the public and private sectors to share information about malicious actors and attack tactics used across different industries. The development of threat intelligence databases and the integration of automated response systems will enable improved defense capabilities against advanced attacks.

OT cybersecurity compliance and regulation is increasing worldwide, with new legislation requiring organizations to meet stricter standards for critical infrastructure security. Regulations such as IEC 62443, the NIS2 Directive, and the NIST Cybersecurity Framework set specific requirements for access management, network protection, and incident response. As governments and regulatory agencies tighten OT security mandates, organizations will need to adapt their cybersecurity strategies to comply with these frameworks and avoid penalties.

Incident response automation is an emerging trend in OT cybersecurity, with the aim of reducing reaction time to attacks and minimizing the impact on industrial operations. Organizations are adopting security orchestration and automation solutions that enable immediate containment actions when a threat is detected. These solutions can isolate compromised devices, block suspicious IP addresses, and automatically trigger recovery protocols, reducing the need for human intervention and speeding up incident response.

The development of secure hardware for industrial environments is a growing trend, with manufacturers designing devices that integrate advanced security mechanisms from the start. Hardware security modules make it possible to protect credentials and encryption keys within devices, preventing them from being extracted or manipulated by attackers. Additionally, secure boot systems ensure that device firmware has not been altered before being put into operation, reducing the risk of tampering attacks in the supply chain.

Private 5G networks are emerging as a solution to improve secure connectivity in industrial environments, providing higher speed and lower latency in communication between OT devices. However, deploying 5G in critical infrastructures requires a security approach that ensures authentication of connected devices, traffic encryption, and network segmentation to prevent unauthorized access. Organizations are exploring strategies to securely integrate 5G into their industrial operations without compromising the stability and resilience of control systems.

OT cybersecurity will continue to evolve in response to the increasing sophistication of attacks and the digitalization of industrial infrastructures. Emerging trends point toward automating detection and response, strengthening cloud security, implementing Zero Trust architectures, and developing secure hardware. As organizations adopt these strategies, the resilience of critical infrastructures will increase, reducing the impact of cyberattacks and ensuring operational continuity in an increasingly interconnected world.

Lessons Learned from Cyberattacks in the Industry

Cyberattacks in industry have shown that critical infrastructure and industrial control systems are increasingly attractive targets for attackers with a variety of goals, from disrupting operations to stealing sensitive information. Over the years, several incidents have highlighted vulnerabilities in operational technology and have served as key lessons for strengthening cybersecurity in these environments. Understanding these attacks and learning from them is essential to improving resilience and preventing future incidents.

One of the most emblematic cyberattacks in the industry was the Stuxnet case, discovered in 2010. This malware was specifically designed to affect SCADA systems and PLCs in nuclear facilities, modifying operating parameters without operators noticing. The main lesson of Stuxnet was that industrial systems can be attacked even without an Internet connection, as the malware spread through infected USB devices. This incident highlighted the importance of removable device control and strict network segmentation to prevent the spread of threats between critical environments.

The 2015 attack on Ukraine's power grid was another significant incident that highlighted the vulnerability of power systems to cyberattacks. Using a combination of phishing and malware, attackers gained access to remote control systems at power substations and shut down power to hundreds of thousands of people. They also disabled SCADA systems and attacked communications equipment, making it difficult to restore service. This attack demonstrated the need to restrict remote access to critical systems, implement multi-factor authentication, and strengthen staff training to detect malicious emails.

Ransomware has become one of the most prevalent threats in the industry, as evidenced by the attack on Colonial Pipeline in 2021. In this incident, a group of attackers managed to compromise the company's IT network and encrypted files essential to the management of the pipeline. Although the OT systems were not directly affected, the company decided to stop its operations as a precaution, generating interruptions in the fuel supply. One of the main lessons of this case was the importance of properly segmenting IT and OT networks to prevent an attack on the administrative part from affecting industrial operations. In addition, the incident underlined the importance of having ransomware recovery plans and performing periodic system restoration tests.

In 2021, an attacker managed to remotely access the Oldsmar Water Treatment Plant in Florida and attempted to alter the levels of chemicals used in the drinking water supply. The access was via a poorly configured remote control tool without multi-factor authentication. The quick reaction of an operator prevented the attack from having serious consequences, but the incident demonstrated the importance of securing remote access and monitoring any changes to critical operating parameters in real time.

The attack on the Pétroleos Mexicanos (Pemex) refinery in 2019 exposed the consequences of a cyberattack on an energy infrastructure. A group of attackers deployed ransomware that encrypted key documents and affected access to administrative systems, slowing down the company's operations. Lack of network segmentation and insufficient backup management made recovery slower than expected. This attack underlined the need for well-defined recovery strategies and regular simulations to assess incident response capabilities.

Denial of service attacks have also affected the industry, as was the case with Norsk Hydro in 2019. This aluminium production company suffered a cyberattack that affected its IT and OT systems, generating multi-million dollar losses. The incident forced the company to manually operate many of its production lines, which highlighted the need for contingency plans to maintain operations in the event of technological interruptions. One of the key lessons of this attack was the importance of designing resilient infrastructures, capable of operating in degraded mode without relying entirely on digital systems.

The human factor remains one of the biggest vulnerabilities in industrial cybersecurity. In multiple attacks, attackers have used social engineering tactics to trick employees into accessing credentials. One notable case was the attack on a steel plant in Germany in 2014, where attackers used phishing techniques to gain access to control systems, causing physical damage to the infrastructure. This incident reinforced the need to train staff in identifying threats and to establish strict access policies for industrial systems.

Another important lesson from cyberattacks in industry is the need to continuously monitor activity on OT systems. In several incidents, attackers managed to remain within the network for weeks or even months before being detected. Implementing AI-based anomaly detection tools and real-time monitoring of security events can help identify suspicious behavior before it materializes into an attack.

Regulatory compliance has emerged as a key factor in protecting industrial infrastructures in the wake of multiple cyberattacks. Regulations such as IEC 62443 and the NIST framework have established standards that seek to improve security in OT environments. Many organizations have learned that compliance is not only a regulatory obligation, but also an effective strategy to reduce risk and improve resilience to attacks.

Cyberattacks in industry have left numerous lessons that have contributed to improving security in critical infrastructures. Network segmentation, remote access restriction, multi-factor authentication, continuous monitoring and staff training are some of the most important measures that have emerged from these incidents. The evolution of threats requires organizations to take a proactive approach to protecting their systems, ensuring that security is a priority in every aspect of industrial operation.

Long-Term Safety Strategies in OT Environments

Security in operational technology environments requires a long-term approach that ensures the continuous protection of critical infrastructure and industrial systems. Unlike IT environments, where updating and modernizing systems is a relatively agile process, in OT devices and technologies often have long life cycles and cannot always be updated without affecting operations. This makes it necessary to adopt sustainable security strategies that allow infrastructure to be protected over time, adapting to evolving threats without compromising operational stability.

One of the fundamental pillars of a long-term security strategy in OT is the implementation of a defense-in-depth model. This approach is based on the application of multiple layers of security at different levels of the infrastructure, ensuring that a failure in one layer does not compromise the integrity of the system as a whole. Network segmentation, access control, strong authentication and continuous monitoring are essential elements to minimize risks over time. As threats evolve, this model allows adjustments to be made without the need to completely redesign the security architecture.

Industrial asset lifecycle management is a key aspect of long-term security. Many OT devices were designed without considering current cyber threats and, in some cases, operate with outdated software that cannot be updated without affecting compatibility with other systems. An effective strategy involves identifying critical assets, assessing their risk level, and defining mitigation plans for legacy devices. In some cases, network segmentation and access restriction may be more viable solutions than directly upgrading hardware or software.

Continuous monitoring and early threat detection are essential for a sustainable security strategy in industrial environments. Real-time monitoring allows for the identification of network traffic anomalies, unauthorized access attempts, and unexpected changes in operating parameters. The integration of artificial intelligence and machine learning in monitoring systems has made it possible to improve the detection capacity of advanced attacks and reduce the response time to incidents. An approach based on proactive threat detection strengthens infrastructure resilience without the need for disruptive changes to its architecture.

Updating and patching OT systems is a challenge that must be addressed with a well-defined strategy. In many cases, software and firmware updates cannot be applied immediately due to operational constraints or compatibility issues with legacy systems. To mitigate these risks, a structured vulnerability management program needs to be implemented that includes regular security assessments, testing in controlled environments, and the application of patches in a phased manner. When updating a system is not feasible, compensating measures such as network segmentation, file integrity monitoring, and the use of application whitelisting should be implemented.

Access control and user authentication play a key role in the long-term security of OT environments. Implementing multi-factor authentication and role-based identity management minimizes the risk of unauthorized access. It is critical that access credentials are not shared between multiple operators and that user accounts are periodically reviewed to eliminate unnecessary access. Additionally, access auditing and real-time monitoring allow suspicious behavior to be detected before it becomes an active threat.

Ongoing staff training is a core element of any long-term security strategy in OT environments. As threats evolve, operators, engineers, and system administrators must be prepared to identify and respond to new types of attacks. Conducting simulation exercises, incident response tests, and cybersecurity awareness programs reinforce the security culture within the organization. Training should not only focus on technical teams, but also on decision-makers, ensuring that security is a priority at all levels of the company.

Regulatory compliance and alignment with international security standards are essential aspects to ensure long-term security in OT. Regulations such as IEC 62443, NIST 800-82, and the NIS2 Directive establish specific requirements for the protection of industrial infrastructures. Complying with these regulatory frameworks not only helps strengthen the security of systems, but also facilitates collaboration with suppliers, customers, and government agencies. Conducting regular audits and documenting security processes ensures that the organization maintains an adequate level of protection over time.

Security automation is a growing trend in the long-term protection of industrial environments. Implementing security orchestration and automation tools allows for immediate response to threats, minimizing the need for manual intervention. These solutions can detect unauthorized access attempts, block suspicious IP addresses, and isolate compromised devices in a matter of seconds. Automation also makes it easier to manage security configurations in complex industrial environments, ensuring consistent application of policies across the entire infrastructure.

Collaboration between industrial companies, technology manufacturers and cybersecurity organizations is a key factor in improving long-term security in OT environments. Sharing information on threats, vulnerabilities and best practices helps strengthen the resilience of the entire industrial ecosystem. Creating threat intelligence sharing centers and participating in collaborative security initiatives helps organizations anticipate emerging attacks and take preventive measures before threats materialize.

Designing resilient infrastructure is a critical aspect of long-term security. An organization's ability to operate safely, even in the face of failures or cyberattacks, depends on implementing redundancy in critical systems, effectively segmenting networks, and planning disaster recovery strategies. Conducting business continuity testing and validating response plans ensures that the company can maintain its operations even in crisis scenarios.

Security in OT environments requires a long-term approach based on combining multiple strategies, from network segmentation and strong authentication to continuous training and incident response automation. As threats evolve and industrial infrastructures become more interconnected, organizations must adopt a flexible and scalable security model that ensures systems are protected without compromising operational stability. Implementing a sustainable security strategy allows industrial companies to face the challenges of the future with greater resilience and confidence.

Final Conclusions and Recommendations

Cybersecurity in operational technology has become a fundamental aspect for the protection of critical infrastructures and industrial environments. As digitalization advances, organizations face new challenges arising from the increasing interconnectivity between OT systems and corporate IT networks. The evolution of cyber threats has shown that traditional security approaches are not sufficient to protect industrial systems and ensure operational continuity. It is necessary to adopt proactive strategies, strengthen security controls and foster an organizational culture that prioritizes cybersecurity as a fundamental pillar of the operation.

The integration of security measures in OT environments must consider the particularities of these systems, where availability and stability are priorities. Network segmentation, the implementation of defense-in-depth models and the adoption of the Zero Trust approach allow for reducing exposure to attacks and minimizing the risks associated with unauthorized access. The separation between OT and IT networks is essential to prevent an attack on the administrative infrastructure from impacting industrial control systems.

Continuous monitoring and early threat detection are key factors in protecting industrial infrastructures. Attacks targeting OT environments can remain hidden for long periods before being detected, highlighting the importance of having advanced monitoring solutions based on artificial intelligence and behavioral analysis. Real-time monitoring of network traffic, identification of anomalous patterns, and automated incident response strengthen the organization's resilience to sophisticated cyberattacks.

Authentication and access control represent one of the most critical points in OT cybersecurity. The use of weak credentials, shared accounts, and default configurations remains one of the main causes of security incidents in the industry. Implementing multi-factor authentication, centralized identity management, and segmenting privileges by role minimizes the risk of unauthorized access. In addition, constant access auditing and revocation of unnecessary accounts reduces the attack surface and prevents information leaks.

Ransomware and denial-of-service attacks have proven to be highly disruptive threats in industrial environments. Protection against these types of attacks requires a combination of strategies, including network segmentation, application whitelisting, and the implementation of secure and isolated backups. The ability to recover from an attack is a determining factor in minimizing the impact on operations and ensuring business continuity. Conducting periodic recovery tests allows validating the effectiveness of contingency plans and optimizing restoration times in the event of incidents.

Staff training is an essential aspect of the OT cybersecurity strategy. Human error and social engineering attacks remain one of the main entry points for attackers. Continuous cybersecurity training, attack simulation and awareness of emerging threats can reduce the likelihood of incidents caused by carelessness or lack of knowledge. Security must be a shared responsibility across the entire organization, from plant operators to senior management.

Regulatory compliance and alignment with international standards strengthens an organization's security posture and facilitates the implementation of best practices. Regulations such as IEC 62443, the NIST 800-82 framework, and the NIS2 Directive establish specific requirements for the protection of critical infrastructure and industrial control systems. Adopting these regulatory frameworks not only improves security, but also enables better collaboration with customers, suppliers, and government agencies. Conducting internal and external audits helps identify security gaps and establish continuous improvement plans.

The adoption of new technologies has created opportunities and challenges in OT cybersecurity. Artificial intelligence and machine learning are transforming incident detection and response by automating security processes and identifying threats in real time. Cloud security, the use of private 5G networks, and the expansion of the Industrial Internet of Things require new protection strategies that guarantee the integrity and confidentiality of data in interconnected environments. Implementing end-to-end encryption, device segmentation, and context-based access control are some of the measures needed to protect these new infrastructures.

Long-term security strategies must focus on resilience and incident response capabilities. Disaster recovery planning, redundancy in critical systems, and threat response automation can help minimize the impact of cyberattacks and ensure operational stability. Public-private collaboration, integration of threat intelligence, and the development of secure infrastructures by design are key aspects to improving security in industry.

The future of OT cybersecurity will depend on organizations' ability to adapt to a constantly evolving environment. The sophistication of cyberattacks and the accelerated digitalization of industry require a dynamic approach to risk management and the implementation of security controls. Investment in protective technologies, staff training, and regulatory compliance will be key to ensuring the security of critical infrastructure in the coming years.

Industrial cybersecurity should not be considered as a one-off project, but rather as a continuous process of improvement and adaptation. Regular risk assessment, implementation of protective measures based on best practices and adoption of advanced technologies will enable organizations to meet security challenges in an increasingly interconnected world. Building a strong security culture within the industry is the key to strengthening the resilience of OT systems and ensuring the continuity of operations in the face of emerging threats.